Grand LARSENY

Grand LARSENY

GAVIN LARSEN

Hodder Moa Beckett

ACKNOWLEDGEMENTS

MANY THANKS TO LYNN McCONNELL, cricket writer at the *Evening Post*, who spent many hours shaping the content of *Grand Larseny*. Over the years I have found Lynn to be an objective, honest and knowledgeable cricket writer and he is certainly one of the more respected media guys in the eyes of the players.

The joy of e-mail enabled Lynn to beaver away at my offerings while I was on duty in England, tidying up my spelling mistakes, getting rid of the rubbish and amending my poor grammar. I also have a new-found respect for media deadlines!

Thanks also to Francis Payne for the statistics which appear at the back of the book.

ISBN 1-86958-773-1

© 1999 – original text Gavin Larsen
The moral rights of the author have been asserted

© 1999 – design and format Hodder Moa Beckett Publishers Ltd

Published in 1999 by Hodder Moa Beckett Publishers Limited
[a member of the Hodder Headline Group]
4 Whetu Place, Mairangi Bay, Auckland, New Zealand

Designed and produced by Hodder Moa Beckett Publishers Limited
Edited by Lynn McConnell
Front cover photo: Annelies van der Poel, Wellington
Back cover photo: Andrew Cornaga, Photosport, Auckland

Printed by Griffin Press, Australia

All rights reserved. No part of this publication may be reproduced or transmitted in any form or by any means, electronic or mechanical, including photocopying, recording, or any information storage and retrieval system, without permission in writing from the publisher.

DEDICATION

TO NIGEL AND WENDY HOARE, and Matthew and Graham Roche. During my time having fun and helping the New Zealand cricket team at the World Cup in England, you were going through your own dramas back here in New Zealand, showing your own great courage and spirit. I hope you all enjoy this book.

And many thanks to Karen, Nadia, Corey, and Vanessa. Without the great support of my family, I would have parted company with cricket years ago.

A day after completing *Grand Larseny* my father passed away suddenly and peacefully in his sleep. Unfortunately Dad never got to read even a draft version of the book. In his perfectionist way he wanted to wait for the printed version. Dad, in your own style and at all times, you supported me in my cricketing travels. Thanks for that. And to Mum, you're my greatest supporter. You've got great family and friends who will be with you through these trying times.

Gavin Larsen
Wellington, July 1999

Contents

You're Nicked (And Named)	8
Foreword	11
Tough Times	15
Better Than Before	19
Road To The Cup	23
Let The Games Begin	47
Then There Were Six	81
Semi-Belief	103
Looking Back	123
Jobs For The Boys	127
Meet The Cast	133
Anyone Can Dream	145
True Colours	151
Of Coaches And Captains	159
Moving On Out	173
Stats	175

New Zealand cricketers love to attach nicknames to their team mates. So to help readers work out who's who in 'Grand Larseny', I've set up this nickname reference. Study it carefully before delving too far into the book.

THE '99 WORLD CUP CREW

Geoff Allott	GA, GQ
Nathan Astle	Nath
Carl Bulfin	Bully
Chris Cairns	BA, Cairnsy
Simon Doull	Doully, Spike
Gilbert Enoka	Bert
Stephen Fleming	Flem
John Graham	DJ
Chris Harris	Harry, H
Mark Harrison	Fran, Harry
Matthew Hart	Harty
Matthew Horne	Hornet, Net, The Old Gun
Gavin Larsen	Gav, The Postman
Craig McMillan	Macca
Dion Nash	Nashy, D

YOU'RE NICKED (AND NAMED)

Adam Parore — Raz, Mav
Steve Rixon — Stumper
Ashley Ross — Shotty
Roger Twose — Twosey, The Pimple
Daniel Vettori — Dan, Lucas

OTHER CAST MEMBERS

Stu Bullen — Bomber
Paul Christian — Fletch
Jeff Crowe — Chopper
Martin Crowe — Hogan
Bob Cunis — Cunie
Lee Germon — Germ
Lance Klusener — Zulu
Rod Latham — Bunker
Warren Lees — Wally
James Milne — JD
John Morrison — Mystery
John Murtagh — Murts
James O'Rourke — Jimmy
Patrick O'Rourke — Paddy
Craig Spearman — Spears
Glenn Turner — Turns
Tim Vogel — Voges
Bryan Waddle — Wadds, The Bullfrog
Shane Warne — Warney
Steve Waugh — Tugga
Andy Wilson — Drew
John Wright — Wrig

Foreword
By John Graham

TO REPRESENT YOUR COUNTRY in a World Cup in any sport is possibly the ultimate reward and privilege for a New Zealand sportsman. To do so in cricket, in England, the traditional home of the game, is indeed special. Our players were on the international stage for over a month, competing against the best in the cricketing world. The team played on famous grounds in front of packed houses, often with constant noise from the Asian supporters of our opposition. The pressure of the one-day game on each individual in the team in such a frenetic environment was immense. Each player's personal expectation of success, those of the team and the supporters at home produced particular demands that had to be met if we were going to succeed.

The tournament produced a roller coaster of emotions from the exhilarating highs of wins against Australia and India and the particular demands of the Scotland game, to the disappointing lows against Pakistan and South Africa. The team was gratified to reach the top four in the world at one-day cricket, after all, the West Indies, India, Sri Lanka, England and Zimbabwe had all gone home!

While it was a rich and pleasing experience, such is the positive development of this side, always seeking to do better than before, that we believed we could have gone the whole way and we know that in several games individuals and the team as a unit had not always done themselves justice.

Who better to diary the daily activities, achievements, disappointments and emotions of this New Zealand team's 1999 World Cup than Gavin Larsen. His continued service to New Zealand and Wellington cricket has been exceptional.

Day in and day out he works to the full extent of his abilities, unobtrusively, purposefully and professionally. His success as one of New Zealand's outstanding one-day players comes from his knowing his own game perfectly. It has been a pleasure over the last three years observing him during a training session and he's attended thousands of these over the years. He warms up diligently enjoying the chatter and banter during the stretching exercises and the demands of the fielding skills programme. He hews away at the practice nets at his bowling, perfecting that nagging length, that accurate line and that movement off the seam. He works hard at his batting, knowing that his twenties and thirties towards the end of a one-day innings can be crucial to a New Zealand win. In the match situation as a bowler he hates conceding runs, as a batsman he relishes the opportunities to score, and as a fielder he defends tenaciously with safe hands. He is the consummate professional, committed, conscientious, competitive and consistent. His nickname of 'The Postman' sums him up well, he always delivers!

Off the field Gavin Larsen's contribution to team life is enormous. He is a manager's dream, always on time, always properly dressed, always clean shaven, and always ready to die for the cause. His stable temperament, his common sense, his awareness of what is appropriate, and his good humour ensure his popularity and success as a team member.

Gavin has a passion for the game and a deep understanding of its complexities and he respects the customs and traditions that are unique to cricket. His captain can rely totally on his support and loyalty on and off the pitch, and he is often used at the captain's team meetings to add tactical or motivational

FOREWORD

advice based on his many years at the top level in his sport.

Gav 'The Postman' Larsen is the model international sportsman. He respects his sport, he is a proud New Zealander who knows it is a privilege to represent his country and he always gives of his best.

Who better, then, to tell the story of the New Zealand Cricket Team's 1999 World Cup adventure.

DJ Graham
New Zealand Cricket team manager
Arundel, May 1999

Tough times

DECEMBER 17, 1997. New Zealand v Australia, Carlton and United preliminary match at the MCG. Michael Bevan hits a ball wide of mid-on and I turn to chase. As I begin sprinting, I feel a searing pain in my left foot and know instantly that I'm in big trouble. Somehow I recover the ball, throw it in, then signal to Flem that I need to leave the field. **I hobble off the famous ground, trying not to limp too much in front of the Aussie supporters, and into the changing room where Mark Plummer, our physio, is waiting for me. He examines me, wraps me in ice, and quickly informs me that my game is over. And my tour.**

I had been experiencing foot pain for the previous week – not overbearing, but the sort of pain you play through week in, week out. It had got progressively worse until this moment, when it felt as though someone had rammed a knife through my foot. I was back on the plane to New Zealand the following morning, and immediately headed for an x-ray in Auckland. The specialist there confirmed the worst. I had a stress fracture in my third metatarsal bone, and was placed in a supporting boot, had crutches thrown at me, and told that six weeks was the minimum down time.

In 14 years of first-class cricket I'd only ever done a couple of hamstrings and the calf that kept me out of the last matches of the '96 World Cup. This was my worst injury, particularly with the home season just hitting the busy stage. By late-January, I was ready to begin training. The foot was healed, and I started to up the tempo. **I was jumping out of my skin to get back onto the park and couldn't wait to start playing for Wellington again,** and then to press my chances for inclusion in the New Zealand one-day team for the series against Australia.

Then the back went, and boy, it went. I was bowling in a club game for Onslow against Johnsonville when my lower back, which had been stiff for a couple of weeks, just seized up on me. I could bowl at half-pace maximum and was in excruciating pain. I couldn't believe it. The following week a series of x-rays and scans yet again revealed the worst. A stress fracture to my lower back (the lower left L4/L5 facet joint), and bad degeneration of the vertebrae being, as the specialist said, a result of running in and hurling down 20,000-plus cricket balls over the last 20 years or so.

So that was it, or so I thought. What a way to go out. Retirement had been forced upon me. At that stage I consider that one person, and one person alone, got me through. Gilbert Enoka had recently been appointed the contracted players' official liaison with New Zealand Cricket, and was making great strides with the players. Bert convinced me to let the dust settle, not to make any rash decisions, and to leave all the administrative stuff for him to work through. He was true to his word, talking with me almost every day to check on progress. I soon realised that in my heart I still wanted to play and that I wasn't ready to pull the pin.

As my rehab continued throughout the winter, Bert was always communicating, being positive, and getting me to pull in the reins if I was getting ahead of myself. When I missed being ready for both the Commonwealth Games and the Dhaka world tournament, I felt negative again, but Bert just kept smiling, kept me positive and kept me looking ahead to the next goal, which became the home season.

I had one little motivation tool during this period. It was provided to me by Lynn McConnell, cricket writer at the

Evening Post. Lynn and I go way back and I respect him immensely as a cricket writer. In fact, he has been extremely helpful in assisting me to pull this book together. I know he'll smile when he reads this. He wrote a review of the 97/98 one-day season and produced a player report. Mine went like this:

> **GAVIN LARSEN**
> Regrettably one of the casualties of the season with stress fractures to a foot and his back. Was missed, although some satisfaction in reaching 100 one-day internationals. Tough road now to force his way back into the team.
> ***Evening Post* points : 4**

Cheers Lynn, but fancy writing me off! I cut the piece out, stuck it in my diary and onto my PC at home, places I knew I would see it every day through my rehab.

There were more downs than ups through this period, but I kept gritting my teeth, training hard and attempting to keep positive. At one stage I was away on a New Zealand Cricket roadshow and was in Gisborne. I went out for a road run with Hornet, and felt great until the next morning. **The pain was back. I was just gutted, talked with Bert and headed straight to Wellington. Again, I nearly tossed the towel in.** It recovered quite quickly that time and I can tell you I've done no road running since.

Nashy had suffered a similar injury a couple of years earlier and I'd heard that he discovered a new method of training. I was willing to try anything to assist my comeback, so had a yarn with Nashy. Body Control Pilates is the method, and I tracked down the studio and went to my first session with a degree of apprehension. I needn't have worried. My instructor, Sefulu, was brilliant and I am now convinced that the main reason I was successful in my comeback was due to Body Control Pilates. It's all about strengthening and improving the flexibility in the 'powerhouse' region of the body, the abdominals, the gluts, the abductors, the hamstrings and quads. When we did the initial testing, I couldn't believe how

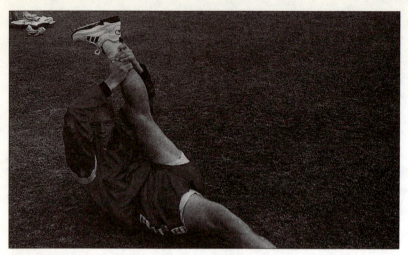
And who says old men aren't flexible?

unbalanced my body had become because of that crazy job called bowling. Sefulu and I worked hard for six months and in time my strength and flexibility had improved out of sight. I'd recommend it to anyone.

In my role as a Hillary Commission Ambassador, I do quite a bit of work with elite sports students in the colleges. Part of the message I leave with these young athletes is for them to question their own levels of commitment, their desire and determination to get the very best out of themselves. I also stress how important setting goals and targets is and putting personal systems in place to help themselves achieve their ambitions. Managing disappointments and setbacks is another area that we cover. It was all so pertinent to me, and as I talked to these students throughout the winter, I'm sure the messages helped me as much as they hopefully helped them.

So I made it. First with the mighty Onslow (or the not-so-mighty as it proved – we were woeful and got relegated), then with Wellington through Cricket Max and the Shell Cup, and then the moment that thrilled me. Re-selection for New Zealand and a chance to renew acquaintances with Tendulkar, Dravid, Azharuddin and Co at Taupo. There was a hint of rust, but it was a start!

Better Than Before

OUR GOOD SHOWING AT the World Cup didn't just happen. Planning started 12 months earlier, in May 1998 when the initial World Cup squad of 30 met at the NZC Academy based at Lincoln University, just out of Christchurch.

The occasion was purely a planning and preparation opportunity, but what a great idea. It was co-ordinated by Gilbert Enoka. It was an opportunity for the squad members to meet as a unit, and for the new management team to outline their expectations and to formulate a vision and series of goals for the upcoming season.

The camp kicked off with a quite inspirational video that Bert had pulled together. It was entitled *England 1999*, our ultimate goal at the end of a number of voyages the team would embark on through a season which would include the Commonwealth Games, the Dhaka one-day tournament in Bangladesh, and the Indian and South African tours of New Zealand. The video began by showing team photographs of all previous NZ teams who had toured England, along with their test match win/loss statistics. **A clip of Robin Williams talking to a group of students in the movie 'Dead Poets Society' followed, with Williams emotionally informing the lads that their predecessors would be stressing 'carpe diem' – urging them to 'seize the day'.** Ex-New Zealand greats such as Bert Sutcliffe, Sir Richard Hadlee and Ian Smith then provided their thoughts on the value of the silver fern.

Bert Enoka (right)... an inspiration to the class of '99.

The video ended with a montage of action shots of the current squad at their best, taking on and bettering the opposition – with the last frames leaving the squad with what would become the team's pledge for the next year. 'BTB' is what it is all about. We want to be 'Better Than Before'. Better in everything we do – our performance, our preparation, our dealings with our team-mates and management, in anything that may play a part, no matter how small, in what we want to ultimately achieve.

> **THE PLEDGE**
> *Gather ye rose buds while ye may. Old time is but a flying.*
> *Honest effort day by day will keep our flag a flying.*
> *Loyalty to my performance and to my mates*
> *Will etch into history significant dates.*
> **BTB**

Chris Harris became the official custodian of the pledge, and to make the pledge something very special it was decided that at the end of every one-day international or test win, Harry would stand and formally state the pledge. It was great to see that Harry had to stand a few times through the 98/99 season.

When the special tape ended, the lights came back on. You could sense the excitement in the room. It was deadly quiet and Bert let the moment sink in.

I had been a bit negative with my stress fracture in my lower back and had been flicking retirement thoughts through my mind. It was this session of Bert's that made up my mind. I wanted to be part of the team again. I wanted to get the ball back in my hand there and then.

The squad then broke off into groups to come up with a new set of values to be used and reinforced through the new season. These values were signed off by the squad as a whole and were:

Pride:	in everything we do.
Attitude:	never say die in both good times and bad.
Integrity:	saying you will do something and doing it.
Honesty:	to ourselves and with each other.
Consistency:	in effort, performance, and application of systems.
Commitment:	to the Fern and to our vision.
Respect:	for each other and the traditions of the past.
Carpe diem:	Seize the day.
Enjoyment:	the journey is as important as the destination.
BTB:	Better Than Before.

I left the camp committed to giving myself every opportunity to recover from the injury and make the team again. I was really excited by the infrastructure that now surrounded the team, undoubtedly the best since I started playing. DJ Graham was a strong manager with whom the guys got on really well. Stumper was fashioning one of NZ's better coaching win/loss records, and Ashley Ross, the team's technical adviser, was adding great value with his bio-mechanics and skills background.

But the key guy, I felt, was Bert. He pulled everything together so well. It is rare to walk past Bert's room on tour and not see him tapping away at some scheme on his laptop.

So the foundations were well laid for all of us. I remember Nashy, at one stage, saying something along the lines of, 'Guys, there aren't any excuses now. Let's get out there and play some good cricket and win.' How true.

Road To The Cup

Saturday, April 24

THE BRIERLEY CRICKET ACADEMY, or the HPC (High Performance Centre) as it's affectionately known. Our base for the next eight days, a final preparation opportunity before we wing it to England.

The squad of 15, plus standby players (Bell, Drum, Croy, O'Connor, Stead) – Brooke Walker couldn't make it through personal circumstances – arrived at lunchtime and got down to business. Bert presented each player with a tour diary and planner which takes us right through to the World Cup final on June 20. As usual no stone was left unturned by Bert – the document was about 80 pages thick!

DJ Graham gave a stirring speech to the squad on the importance of the next couple of months. He stressed the thrill of playing on the world stage and the obvious point that World Cups come around only every four years. He said that we must seize the opportunity in front of us, that it is a very even playing field in terms of favouritism, and that the team that was best prepared and wanted it the most would emerge champions.

Bert showed the squad a small box that was to be the team's Treasure Chest for the duration of the Cup. Each squad member was asked to add one item to it by the time we boarded the plane for England. He started the ball rolling with

Fresh kit, fresh dreams... the 1999 World Cup squad. I'm standing third from right.

a compass, saying that at times the ship may veer a little off course, and that the compass should be a reminder to do whatever is necessary to lock the ship back on to its target.

The afternoon was spent in the HPC on our favourite task – fitness testing! It was a pretty comprehensive two and a half hours that included the old favourite Beep Test, a 20m sprint, a 'Run 3' – running a three with bat, pads and gloves, **a fat test (that always scares a couple – I never could get rid of those love handles!),** a flexibility test, and then, to finish it off, a new one for me. It's called a RHIT (Repetitive High Intensity Test), basically six 30-second shuttle runs at full speed. By the fourth one the head was spinning, all oxygen had left the body and the lactic acid had blown up the legs. I heard later that guys have been known to vomit at the end of this one. Our fitness trainer Dougal Steven said that part of this test was not only to check out anaerobic capacity, but also to see who could do the hard yards. The overall fitness was pretty good, and it was great also to see Cairnsy, Flem, and Macca sweating it out after their lay-offs with injury. Twose and Larsen, the two Wellington boys, managed to urge each other on through the afternoon!

ROAD TO THE CUP

Sunday, April 25

The Chris Harris Benefit Match
THE GODS DIDN'T SMILE on Harry today, offering up a cold, wet Jade Stadium. Unfortunately for H, that meant the punters didn't turn up in their droves, and the boys felt for him as he is a real deserving beneficiary. A legend down there in red-and-black country for sure. Talking of Cantab support, I remember a one-day international I played at Jade Stadium a couple of years ago, when I got great support from the terraces as I fielded in front of them. It was a different story the next week, though, when I donned the Wellington colours for a Shell Cup match against their beloved Canterbury team. **I was now the villain, and was yelled at and sledged as I fielded in exactly the same spot. Who says they all wear red-and-black eye-patches!**

Harry's match was a 45-over affair, North v South, and played as seriously as possible given the conditions and state of the ground, which was definitely set up for Super 12 rugby. The South eventually prevailed and it was a useful shakedown after about three weeks off. There were a few stiff bodies around, though, particularly after the fitness test yesterday.

Monday, April 26

OUTFITTING AT NZC HEADQUARTERS. A bit like Christmas with all the new kit dished out. The team has really strong $$ penalties for wearing non-sponsor apparel. As a consequence we are now decked out with really smart casual gear. **NZC's advice to us is to bring just our socks and undies and they'll provide the rest. Makes quite a sight at the airport when you arrive!**

A long queue also forms outside CEO Chris Doig's office this morning as the guys want to dot the i's and cross the t's with their NZC contracts before we head off. I guess Chris breathes a sigh of relief when our plane finally leaves the tarmac.

Doully's donation to the Treasure Chest is a Silver Fern. Doesn't need a lot of explaining.

GRAND LARSENY

Tuesday, April 27

WARM-UP MATCH ON Lincoln Green (right next to the HPC). It was a pretty sporting wicket that helped the quicks and kept the batters honest. Also helping the bowlers was the fact that we used the English Duke ball that we would apparently be using in the World Cup. If we used the same ball, the bat manufacturers were going to have nightmares. Six bats were broken during the match. **The ball was like a small shot-put, incredibly hard with a really pronounced seam. It was stamped on one side 'Dukes 1991': the batch they sent us was eight years old.** Twosey seemed to remember that around that time in England they were experimenting with the balls used in county cricket. We are hoping that 1991 was a 'bad' batch, and that the World Cup ball is a bit friendlier. If that's true, then we've been gloved by the tournament organisers who have obviously sent any old ball for us to prepare with. I wonder if the ABs would get dud balls to train with before a World Cup?

Macca's had a full number two haircut. A couple of days earlier he was pretty proud that he hadn't had a cut for about a year. DJ's obviously been in his ear!

My donation to the treasure chest is a watch. A watch measures time and I reckon that how we go about organising and using time is going to be a crucial component in our success.

Other donations included a chain from Cairnsy. Bert has pulled a document together summarising each of the donations, and his summary of the chain was great. **This chain is made up of many individual links - each link looks the same, but they each have strengths and weaknesses. For this chain to be a chain all the links need to combine in a way that creates something superior. The chain is only a chain if all the individual links do their job.** Adam donated a pair of batting gloves, saying that they signified the times when we had to 'take the gloves off', to fight it out. Macca threw in a golf ball and pack of cards, saying that we needed to make sure we didn't lose sight of the need to have fun. To get the balance right between work and play. Quite profound for a young fella.

The annual Shell Awards dinner was held tonight in Christchurch. Nath cleaned up most of the major men's awards, needing a truck to cart all his silverware home. His speeches also became shorter and more incoherent as the night wore on! Was the last opportunity for the boys to really let their hair down before we headed off.

```
Wednesday, April 28
```

A WATER DAY. FIRST, a recovery session in the QEII pool, then into the bus and off to the Hanmer Springs for an afternoon of R and R. Half the squad hit the golf course (as usual, the team including the Fleming/Astle duo won – huge accusations of cheating again!), the rest of us spent the afternoon in the hot pools. Fantastic spot. Hornet just wouldn't get out. After four hours of boiling his carcass, his head resembled a cross between a beetroot and a lobster. He's a real hot water man. Don't ever be next in line when Hornet's in the shower. There's nothing surer than the hot water will have run out.

Another set of treasure chest items. Twosey's addition was our National Anthem. Pride was his main word as he added it to the chest. **A betting slip was donated by Harry, signifying the times during this tournament that we will need to take a gamble.** He mentioned that gambles should be well-calculated risks. Nashy added an Aqua Cooler (a cooling neck-tie that hangs around your neck), for use when there was a need to keep your cool. And GA threw in a corkscrew, for when the job is finally done.

```
Thursday, April 29
```

WEIGHTS CIRCUIT AT THE Les Mills Gym. GA always impresses and inspires me. He's a 100 per cent man in all endeavours (always right up there in the beep test with Adam and Shayne O'Connor, which is no mean feat for a big fella). At 9am at Les Mills, he's there giving it heaps and leading the way.

The afternoon sees open wicket practice on Lincoln Green to get a few more overs under the belt, then Twosey and I spend an hour in the indoor net. Twosey's put his medium-pacers on the shelf. He's sure his huge ripping off-spinners are his bowling future.

Further donations to the Treasure Chest included Fran throwing some super-glue in, saying that we'll need to stick together as a team through thick and thin. **Flem added a small golden heart – dedicated to the wives and partners left behind. A caring guy!** And Gary Stead threw in his lucky 20-cent coin (10 out of 12 tosses won for Canterbury with it), saying that with Flem's abysmal tossing record for the Black Caps last season, he was more than welcome to use it.

Friday, April 30

OUR FINAL SHAKEDOWN MATCH at Lincoln Green. The rock hard Dukes balls were put back on the shelf in favour of our normal Kookaburra to save our bats! Another good blowout, but it's fair to say most minds are already on the plane to England.

On the social note, the squad has been split into four mini-teams for events throughout the tour. After the match, a formal presentation of the official team singlets is made by each of the four captains.

The mini-teams are:

The Parramatta Eels
1. Daniel Vettori (c)   (with Brett Kenny on his back)
2. Gavin Larsen   (with Mick Cronin on his back)
3. Steve Rixon   (with Ray Price on his back)
4. Nathan Astle   (with Peter Sterling on his back)
5. Simon Doull   (with Eric Growth on his back)

The background to the Eels centres around Dan Vettori, who supports the Eels in the NRL and stirring it up a bit with Steve Rixon, who is a St George Dragons supporter. Dan then picked the great championship winning team of 1986 to base his team on. Don't know how he remembers that team; he'd only just been born! The Eels are a beautifully-balanced team, full of flair, match-winners, and guys to do the hard yards.

The Spice Boys
1. Roger Twose (c)   (Porky Spice)
2. DJ Graham   (Old Spice)
3. Matthew Horne   (Horney Spice)
4. Craig McMillan   (Sugar 'n Spice)
5. Gilbert Enoka   (Smiley Spice)

This unit will spend so much time worried about their appearance that they'll forget about the competition. Not only will the mirrors get a battering, but they'll over-analyse everything. Will Old Spice be the weak link?

The Hart Throbs
1. Matthew Hart (c)
2. Chris Cairns
3. Chris Harris
4. Ashley Ross
5. Carl Bulfin

There's a rift in this camp already with Cairnsy gutted with Harty over the bland white singlets that the captain pulled together. No thought, no innovation, no flair – definitely sums up the Hart Throbs! In-fighting will be the death of this team.

The Stunned Mullets
1. Geoff Allott (c)
2. Stephen Fleming
3. Mark Harrison
4. Adam Parore
5. Dion Nash

The Stunned Mullets could be the early TAB favourites as they are captained by the inspirational 100 per cent man. **Could be the dirty team, the sledgers, and this could really work against them. Arrogance will undoubtedly be the Stunned Mullets' Achilles heel!**

Should be a lot of fun, and I'm sure everyone's competitive streak will emerge once competition starts.

New Zealand Cricket threw a dinner that evening for the World Cup squad, the Academy guys based at Lincoln, and the New Zealand Cricket administration. The first function of this type that I'd ever been to, and it was really good to be able to put faces to the names that we deal with over the phone regularly during the season.

Saturday, May 1

AFTER A RECOVERY SESSION at QEII pool, the squad was addressed by Christopher Doig, and he wished everyone the best for the upcoming tour. Chris is a most eloquent, articulate, and emotional communicator, a reflection in part of his previous occupation as a professional opera singer, I guess. And he is a real professional, a fact that he attempts to drive home and instil into the contracted players at every opportunity. He's also a very persuasive negotiator, a fact not lost on many of the guys as they worked through contract issues over the last week.

From a players' perspective, Chris has been seen as the driving force behind many of the positive changes within New Zealand Cricket over the last three years. These include the advent of the Lincoln-based Academy, a move towards minimum payment scales for first-class cricketers, the introduction of Conference Cricket, and annual tours to New Zealand by overseas 'A' teams (e.g. Bangladesh A, Pakistan A, and, this season, England A). **From a New Zealand player's viewpoint, the potential to earn bigger bucks is there now as long as you make the team,** the team wins a fair proportion of matches, and you perform consistently. There is now a top superannuation scheme in place to assist players once their playing days are over, and income protection is well in place to cover loss of earnings for injured players. The management team of Stumper, DJ, Bert, Shotty, and Fran that surrounds the team really completes the jigsaw.

After Chris' address, we headed to Jade Stadium for our formal World Cup photo. We were all decked out in our number ones (suit and tie), **those with no socks took their spot in the back row** and Twosey, who had only a short-sleeved white shirt, was happy that it was a jackets-on photo. Team photos are always an opportunity for the boys with a sense of humour. Bully kindly let Shotty know that he had dandruff, and naturally the voice of the one and only Chris Harris was heard throughout.

Chris Doig... driving force behind many positive changes.

The final contributions to the treasure chest were made today. **Nath added a one dollar coin, saying that we'd end up with a few of these if we went all the way.** Dan's donation was great. He threw in a knife, advising that if you wanted to criticise someone, stab them in the belly, not the back – do it to their face and not behind their back – and pick the time when you want to use the knife. And he's only 20 years old! Harty added what he called an Attitude Story. It was a story that he had stumbled across, and its message was to stay positive in the face of adversity.

Sunday, May 2

I NEVER REALLY THOUGHT I'd see this moment. I'm writing this sitting in the Air NZ lounge at Christchurch Airport ready to board NZ27 to Singapore and then on to London Heathrow. For me it's been a long year and a half, with plenty of ups and downs, and emotional highs and lows. **After almost pulling the pin on cricket owing to my back injury, I'm ecstatic now to be departing New Zealand for the 1999 World Cup.**

The guys are all relaxed, many reading the Sunday papers (passing comment on the sporting articles as usual), and having a quiet drink and snack. Expectant. We are embarking on what has to be the major highlight and opportunity for any international cricketer, to compete and hopefully succeed in the World Cup. Our chances? Well, the way I see it, this World Cup involves the most even field yet. South Africa stand out, and Pakistan are dangerous. But no-one outside of New Zealand rates our chances at all. That's a great start for us. We have our top players all fit again (and they are game-breakers too – Flem, Cairnsy, and Macca) and, touch wood, injuries won't play a major part over the next couple of months. Our structures, systems and disciplines are all in place and are now second nature to the guys. We've also progressed past that 'young and inexperienced' tag that has been bandied around the last couple of years. So, who knows? **Marry in some exceptional individual performances, a team that will fight every inch of the way, a ball that hopefully bounces our way, and heaps of Kiwi passion and pride and we could do a lot of damage. Hopeful? You bet!**

Monday, May 3

TOUCHED DOWN AT HEATHROW at midday. It's taken just on two days of travelling. In fact, Shotty, who travelled separate to the team left New Zealand seven hours after us and arrived in London an hour or so before us. Emirate Air are the official travel sponsors of the World Cup, so to keep the organisers and sponsors happy, we had an eight-hour stopover in Singapore before we could connect with an Emirates flight. Then another three hours to endure in Dubai, as Emirates don't fly Singapore-London direct. The South Africans were on our Dubai-London leg, and their travel took 20 hours when their direct flight normally takes 10 hours. Shame! Pretty damn tiring all up, though.

The tournament organisers seem switched on. We get whisked through immigration and our baggage is cleared quickly. We've got over 70 pieces of checked-in luggage. On top of that, each guy has two cabin pieces – a suit carrier and hand-bag. Flem and Stumper are raced into a press conference and then we are on our way to Southampton. Because of the excellent motorway system, we travel everywhere in England by bus. Our driver, Eric, stays with the team for the duration of the Cup, along with Kevin, the baggage man, and Ray, our liaison man. **Cairnsy reckons Eric looks like Doully – so he's been nicknamed Spike's Dad!**

It's one and a half hours from Heathrow to Southampton, taking the M25 (the three-lane ring-road motorway that orbits Greater London), then the M3 that heads south. Travelling the British motorways is certainly a different experience than State Highway One Wellington to Kaitaia. The volume of traffic makes you realise what a quiet little country New Zealand is.

The boys were pretty shagged on arrival, so to stop anyone heading straight to bed, we popped down to a local Common and had a bit of a jog and a quiet game of touch rugby. Was all a bit lethargic. **It was a Bank Holiday Monday (a national holiday), and it was interesting to see the Common full of people having fun, and baring their lily-white bodies to a watery sun. Gave the boys a bit of a laugh.**

Before crashing out in the evening, most of the guys met in the bar and enjoyed a quiet pint or two of Caffreys Bitter. When in Rome do as the Romans do.

GRAND LARSENY

Tuesday, May 4

FIRST PIECE OF CUP controversy. Alan Donald, South Africa's white lightning, was featured in the *Daily Express* tabloid saying he had no respect whatsoever for Brian Lara as a person. **He was quite critical of Lara, noting incidents that occurred in their recent test series and really didn't hold back at all. Could be an interesting match if the Windies take on South Africa at any stage.** He also, in a general way, criticised umpiring standards, saying that the South Africa board in the same test series paid win bonuses to his team even though they hadn't won because their board reckoned that umpiring had affected the results of the matches. That certainly wouldn't happen in New Zealand!

A few of the guys (Twosey, GA, Fran, Adam, Nashy, myself) are looking to use e-mail to keep in touch with people back home. So we hunted down a cyber café in Southampton and spent an hour sending off a few e-mails. It's quite interesting – if you buy a coffee you get the rental rate at half-price. Even cricket touring has turned into a high-tech affair now with a few of the boys carrying laptops around with them!

Our team room was wall-to-wall with cricket bats, 250 of them, and each one had to be signed by the team. After 250 autographs, it feels like RSI is setting in. **Nath stole a march on everyone and turned up early. He completed his signing first, and then found out he had used the wrong pen.** Nath is always so neat, organised, and prepared, so he took a bit of stick for that muck-up.

Late afternoon we had our first practice at the County Ground, home of Hampshire CCC and venue of our warm-up match on Saturday against Hampshire, and our third World Cup match, against the Windies. A lovely looking English county ground, picturesque with real traditional surroundings, and excellent practice facilities. You just can't help but feel like playing cricket.

ROAD TO THE CUP

Hornet working his way through 250 autograph bats.

```
Wednesday, May 5
```

MOST OF THE BOYS had trouble sleeping – the jet-lag was still hanging around. Bully was wide awake at 5am so went out for a run. Not the sort of thing yours truly would do.

On the bus to practice, Flem mentioned that *The Sun* newspaper had made us their favourites to win the World Cup. **That made us all laugh, the sleaziest, least reputable, most sensational daily tabloid installing us as their preference.**

A few reckoned we should get a Page three girl each if we won! On a betting note (and we all know that cricketers never bet), we popped into a local Ladbrokes betting shop to sneak a look at the World Cup odds. We just aren't rated. In our group, we're at 16/1 to make the Super Sixes, firmly behind Aussie, who are at evens, the Pakis at 2/1, and the Windies at 7/2. If only we had a spare tenner!

That evening we were back into the number ones for a formal function hosted by Hampshire CCC. These are the evenings that most of the boys grin and bear. Heaps of yarning to committee members and older supporters, a quick plate of finger food, formal speeches from the HCCC Chairman and DJ, and then the squad members introduced to the audience. One of the Southampton City Councillors welcomed us and was obviously a bit nervous. Weighed down by his council chains around his neck, he started badly by telling us 'not to go out tonight, you've got a game tomorrow' – our game is on Saturday and today is Wednesday! **He then talked about the 'recent future' and the boys couldn't resist a laugh at him. Think he'd had a few pints after work.**

There's no doubt that Liverpool are the greatest soccer team in the world. Tonight they were playing the pretenders from Lancashire, Manchester United, and they were about to put a dent in United's championship hopes. Macca wouldn't wear this, though, being a United supporter, so a quiet 10 pounds was up for grabs. Down 2-0 halfway through the second spell, I had a wee sweat on, but the Merseyside gods dug deep and scored the equaliser with two minutes to play.

Thursday, May 6

AFTER LAST NIGHT'S SOCCER result, it was good to run into Macca today. The boys were given the day off training. Flem, myself and Harty decided to get in a bit more practice, though, so hit the nets at 9am. **It was England in May as I remember it: damp and cold, and 10 degrees max.** There had been a bit of rain overnight, the ground was wet and overall it wasn't very pleasant. You don't see cricketers training in beanies too often!

Most of the other guys topped up on their fitness by hitting the gym or going for a run. There's one thing about cricket – you have to grab every opportunity to keep up the fitness levels. Half a dozen of the squad were part of a local golf day, and Dan Vettori showed his prowess by being part of the team that came last.

GA, Bully and Adam had a coaching clinic to run for a group of local 14-year-olds. At the end of the practice, GA bowled a few to the local lads. **He showed his competitiveness by first dropping an inswinging yorker onto a batsman's toe, and then next ball banging one in short and getting it up to chest height.** Bully was pictured in the local rag showing a batsman how to play a backward defensive shot. This cracked up the boys because Bully's standard shot to a short ball is a hook or pull.

Friday, May 7

RAIN, RAIN, RAIN. PRACTICE was cancelled, and instead we had a workout in the HCCC gym and utilised the indoor nets for some throwdowns. There's one sure thing about cricket – it's a summer game.

Diet Pepsi and a good book for Flem – what else do you do when the rain's falling?

GRAND LARSENY

The evening before each match we have a Captain's Meeting. It's Flem's opportunity to outline tactics for the match and his thoughts about where we're at as a team. At this meeting Flem stated that we had 150 overs of batting and bowling over the next three games in order to top off our preparation and for the selectors to decide on the right type of team balance to take into the World Cup. For this first match Bully, Harty, Doully and myself sit it out – we get our chance in the next game, against Surrey. A bit of a worry personally as my guess is that the selectors would want the shadow starting World Cup team playing this first match.

We had dinner as a team, checking out Robin Smith's restaurant called *Judges*. Judgey is captain of Hampshire and had a pretty successful career with the England team, and he'd got a great little eating spot in Romsey, a typically quaint English village just out of Southampton. **The boys enjoyed their feed. However, those who chose the cod thought it had been caught six months ago and had been lost in the back of the fridge.**

Saturday, May 8

NEW ZEALAND V HAMPSHIRE AT SOUTHAMPTON
Hampshire   135-6 after 39 overs (rain)
New Zealand   168-2   Win by 8 wickets

A COMFORTABLE WIN FIRST-UP with the bowlers doing a great job. After a bit of rain (surprise, surprise) we had a revised target and Nath, Hornet, Flem and Macca saw us through comfortably with overs to spare. A good confidence booster to kick off the tour.

One breed of supporter you just can't get away from over here is the autograph hunter. They are everywhere – at the ground, at training, outside the hotel, outside the team bus... you name it, they're there. The strange thing is that unlike New Zealand, where most of the autograph hunters are youngsters, over here they are almost all adults. They all have sheets with the players' names already typed out nicely, and they are almost frantic in their efforts to make sure they catch everyone. I'm sure today I signed for one particular guy about a dozen times. It can get pretty frustrating. However, as Bert points out, signing autographs is an 'is', not an 'is not' – it doesn't take much time, it's good PR, and comes with the territory. Definitely the link between players and the public is managed by the way we conduct ourselves at times like this.

We were straight on to the bus and off to London (two hours up the road). **Harty and I killed the time by taking on Flem and Nath at euchre. At 10 quid a game, it ebbed and flowed, and as we pulled into the Kensington Royal Garden Hotel, the honours were even.** The boys were looking forward to hitting London. A few shot out straight away to catch up with mates, and the rest of us headed for Covent Garden for a few quiet ones. Bryan Waddle, who arrived in London today, joined us for a beer and it was good to catch up with him and see that he was as talkative as ever. Ray, our liaison guy, also met up with Wadds and had no hesitation in producing his own nickname for the radio man – 'The Bullfrog'. The boys loved it.

```
Sunday, May 9
```

10.30AM. RECOVERY SESSION at the Dolphin Hotel where they had a neat indoor swimming pool. Must have startled all the locals who were enjoying a casual Sunday morning paddle with their families, when suddenly 15 cricketers jumped in and started pumping out lengths. **Knocked into a couple from Khandallah – five minutes from where I live – who now live in London. The world's certainly not that big a place.**

After every match we have a formal debrief. It's all part of thoroughly analysing our performance, to tidy up any loose ends, and to begin preparation for our next match. Bert facilitates the meeting and by mid-afternoon a two-page debrief sheet is slipped under everyone's door. Stumper says

Bert is slowly killing off all the trees. This particular debrief covered the following key points:
1. **The ball** – its general condition, hardness, amount of swing and seam gained. Looking after the ball, and the amount of reverse swing.
2. **The pitch** – moisture content and amount of movement. Bat first v bowl first policy. Durability and amount of spin gained.
3. **The weather** – the inevitable delays for rain, and managing these down times. Awareness of the run chase calculations after rain.
4. **General** – to read certain 'positive' articles out of the paper, which summarised all the competing teams and also an article by Mike Atherton on potential team tactics that could be employed throughout the World Cup. **Bert even reminded the boys that today was Mother's Day. Whoops! If you end up reading this, Mum, have a very happy Mother's Day for May 9.**

Tomorrow's a crucial day for me. After missing selection for the first match, this could be a one-off chance for myself, Doully, Bully and Harty. We'll need to show some form as I guess the selectors will want something close to the first World Cup XI to play in the final of our warm-up matches, against Sussex.

Had an optional practice in mid-afternoon at The Oval, the venue of our next match. After you get off the bus, you wind your way up three flights of stairs before hitting the changing rooms, which have a simply fantastic view right over the ground.

Hornet was in front of me and as he hit the top he simply said, 'Shit!' It really is a great sight. I think it's got to be the most recognisable ground in the world with the huge gas works that dominate the surroundings. Doully completely disagrees. He goes for Newlands in Cape Town, which has Table Mountain as its backdrop. Had a good one-hour net on this great ground.

Monday, May 10

NEW ZEALAND V SURREY AT THE OVAL
New Zealand   329-6
Surrey   220 all out   Win by 109 runs

WE BATTED FIRST AND after losing Hornet for a blob, Macca entered stage right. Fifty-odd balls later he departed stage left, 86 runs next to his name. It was a truly great big-hitting innings. He really is something special, and almost impossible to bowl to when in that sort of mood. **He was out reverse-sweeping the leg-spinner, a really poor option (and I know Stumper and Flem are livid with him and will tell him so), but that really sums up the way he approaches his cricket.** Bryan Waddle even said that he blew a double hundred! If Macca could just minimise those really high-risk shots he plays (and even defend a ball or two – we bowlers do bowl the odd good ball, Mac) then he has the ability to be one of the very best. His bowling last season in New Zealand summed up his competitive spirit. Mac bowls quite a heavy ball, and he decided that bowling bouncers was the way to go. So he did, ball after ball, over after over, all the while letting every batsman know how badly they were playing the short ball.

We were 120-odd off our first 15 overs, and ended with 329-6. In reply Surrey got away to a quick start, but after they lost a few wickets they really just went through the motions. The bowling was sound without us being under huge pressure, all the bowlers will have their fingers crossed that they get one more chance on Wednesday at Arundel.

Tuesday, May 11

WE ARRIVED LATE LAST night at Arundel after travelling down from The Oval after the match. We're at the centuries-old Stakis Avisford Hotel, which was once the home of Sir George Montague, Admiral and friend of Lord Nelson. A really

Macca... a bit to learn about reverse sweeps and team laundry.

majestic spot, set in 62 acres of gardens and parkland. It even has its own 18-hole golf course – not a great surprise that some of the guys took advantage of this.

Swim, debrief, and afternoon off to re-charge the batteries for tomorrow. Bert used the debrief as an opportunity to remind everyone to keep managing their state of mind. He reminded us to maintain a day-by-day/game-by-game focus, to keep trusting our own personal systems of preparation and review, and to stay true to these through good times and the bad. It was a short but pertinent session and a great checkpoint for the guys by Bert.

Macca is our team laundry man. His job is to strike up the best possible deal in each location to help everyone's laundry bill, and

usually we get a bag of washing done for about 15 quid. He proudly announced on arrival here that we'd also been given 20 per cent off. We thought nothing of it until the laundry arrived, very clean and well-pressed, with shirts on coat hangers. My bill was for £45, about $130. That was for one bag of socks, underpants, t-shirts and playing gear! Mine was nothing though. Hornet got pinged for 87 quid – you should have seen the look on his face. Macca ducked for cover and couldn't be found anywhere. Fortunately Bert and Kevin, our luggage man, finally got face-to-face with the Chief Manager and after negotiation (signed cricket bats being the carrot) the laundry was given to us free of charge. Needless to say, Macca will be a little more thorough at our next destination.

In the evening we shot down to one of the local pubs, had a meal, and watched the crucial Arsenal v Leeds footie match on a big screen. The passion that soccer generates over here is quite remarkable. It really is like a religion. **Here we are southwest of London, no local team involved, yet all the locals were screaming their lungs out** (must admit we got a bit involved too). In terms of winning the Premiership, the locals were split in their support of either Arsenal or Man U (the scum!). Final result? 1-0 to Leeds and I'm gutted as there could be a few quid heading Macca's way.

Wednesday, May 12

NEW ZEALAND V SUSSEX AT ARUNDEL
Sussex   219-7
New Zealand   220-2   Win by 8 wickets

OUR LAST WARM-UP MATCH and another really solid performance. The bowling was steady throughout with GA outstanding, and then Macca (with a superb 94), Twosey, and Flem knocking off the runs in real style with nearly 10 overs remaining. Personally it was great to get a run in this final match pre- World Cup and I got through my 10 overs for 35 runs.

At 40/1 just before the start of the tournament, GA was a great bet to become the leading wicket-taker. As betting is banned amongst the players, GA, of course, couldn't take the punt.

There's still a bit to work on at practice, but at least I've left my name in front of the selectors.

Arundel has to be one of the most pleasant cricket grounds around. It's a real village-green setting, marquees scattered around one side, with the famous Arundel Castle forming part of the backdrop. Plenty of corporates seem to make it a day out for staff and clients, and **there was no lack of champagne and cigars floating around. Salmon and prawns were on the players' lunch menu, so it paid to hit the old food queue early.**

After each day's play we complete what we call a Fourth Session. This session takes about half an hour and includes loading up on some carbohydrates (food is organised by management), re-hydrating if necessary (there's always plenty of water and energy drink in the changing rooms), and then a solid period of stretching, Swiss Ball exercises and Theraband work. Therabands resemble large strong rubber bands and are used for strengthening exercises, mainly for the shoulders and arms. This Fourth Session is now second nature to the guys, who just get on and complete their own work at the end of every day's play.

Thursday, May 13

WOKE UP IN THE Posthouse Hotel in Brentwood, about 10km out of Chelmsford, where we play Bangladesh on Monday. Cricket touring's a pretty nomadic lifestyle, particularly when we're in one-day mode. **You seem to be forever jumping on and off the bus, checking into new hotels, and then sussing out the hotel restaurants, bars, laundry, and gym.** Then it's a routine of recovery, debrief, practice, fitness sessions, team meetings, match day, and then back on the bus to begin again. What is nice is when you have a reasonably extended period of time in one spot, like here in Brentwood. You can actually think about unpacking the suitcase and living 'normally' for a few days. One of the bonuses here at the World Cup is that we all get a single room each. You get to spread out a bit and certainly get more privacy. Normally on tour only the captain gets a single, with everyone else sharing.

Obviously you can't practise and have team sessions all day every day, so there is a fair proportion of down-time for the guys. **Everyone has their own way of filling in time to keep the mind and body active and sharp. The team room has a video and TV and a few of the guys are into videos that the social fund fronts for.** Some read a lot, and others are into getting out around the local area (yesterday afternoon Hornet jumped on a train by himself and spent the afternoon shopping in

Chelmsford, and Twosey and GA 'British Railed' it into London to hunt down a Cyber Café so they could surf and drink coffee). Fran is also kept busy with the guys who are carrying little niggles, or want some PM – Preventative Maintenance. As I've already said, some of the guys are also carting laptops around, and are slowly turning themselves into propheads. Harry's got himself a brand new state-of-the-art laptop with all the bells and whistles, which must have cost him quite a few signed One-Day shirts. Might take him a while to learn, though – we had to show him where the on/off button was.

Let The Games Begin

Friday, May 14

AT LAST! GAME ONE of the 1999 World Cup – England, the hosts, v Sri Lanka, the defending champions, at Lord's. You couldn't have scripted a better start. Alec Stewart and Arjuna Ranatunga's famous run-in in Australia last summer spiced the game up nicely, and Shane Warne added fuel to the fire today by writing a bizarre column in *The Times* absolutely bagging Arjuna. Basically he said that the Sri Lankan captain played the game of cricket in a confrontational manner, and that his team as a whole was untrustworthy. Great stuff! **His column was inflammatory throughout, and I know if one of us had written it, he would be missing a match fee or three.**

We watched the opening ceremony while we completed a weights session at a local gym, and the feeling was that it was a bit insipid. Flags unrolled on the ground, a few balloons, smoke, and that was about it. Didn't come close to the 1996 ceremony in Calcutta. The rain didn't help much, but surely the English could have come up with something a bit more inspiring. In the match itself the early drizzle forced the players off a couple of times, but after winning a crucial toss, England went on to a comfortable win. One that will keep their tabloid wolves at bay – for a while at least.

GRAND LARSENY

Saturday–Sunday, May 15–16

A WEEKEND OF PRACTICE before our opening match against Bangladesh. Preparation has gone well and the guys' work ethic has been great. We just want to hit the park now and start competing. The team was named at the Captain's Meeting on Sunday evening, and there was huge internal satisfaction when my name was read out. Competition for the bowling spots had been really strong, with the big factor being what team balance Flem and Stumper were to decide upon. In the end, they went with the additional security of an extra batsman because of the seaming wickets, along with playing an extra seamer and leaving out both the left-arm spinners. **To play in this World Cup had been a big goal for me, the one big reason I decided to work through that long rehab period after I did my back in.** All the hard work has now been worth it and the big thing is to now cement my spot. So the team that has the honour of leading New Zealand into the World Cup opener is: Astle, Horne, McMillan, Fleming, Twose, Cairns, Parore, Harris, Nash, Larsen, Allott.

The non-players are Vettori, Hart, Bulfin, and Doull.

We've done a lot of planning, the preparation has been thorough, and everyone has worked hard at their individual games. The talk stops now though, and to paraphrase, it's time to 'walk the talk'.

Monday, May 17

NEW ZEALAND V BANGLADESH AT CHELMSFORD
Bangladesh   116 all out
New Zealand   117-4   Win by 6 wickets

WE'RE ON THE BOARD. A good game to get out of the way, and two vital points in the bank. Chelmsford was a sell-out and we quickly found out why. It was like playing in the middle of Dhaka. The Bangladeshi support was tremendous,

Typically happy Bangladeshi supporters at Chelmsford.

with every run scored (and there weren't many) or wicket taken being met by a barrage on the drums, horns and whistles. A very noisy day.

Flem won a crucial toss, decided to bowl, and we quickly had Bangladesh in trouble. **GA continued his good form with a couple of early wickets and Cairnsy also bowled well, snaring a couple.** The big man also threw himself around in the field and was pretty fired up all round. Hopefully ominous. With the wicket seaming around a bit, and with Bangladesh looking to regroup, my job was made easier bowling first change after Nashy. Third ball I held onto a caught and bowled, which is pretty rare for me – I've dropped my last three caught and bowleds for NZ. The day before I had done some specific c&b catching practice, with Bert working with me. He quickly claimed this as his first international wicket! I ended with 3-19 off my 10, which even snared me the Man of the Match award. Quietly satisfying.

We struggled though a little with the bat, but still knocked off the total comfortably enough. It wasn't a great wicket, a

Man-of-the-Match against Bangladesh. The champers I won went west after the Aussie game.

bit two-paced and seamed too much for a one-dayer. All in all, we had to be happy to have a couple of points on the board. It was now on to one of our biggies, the Aussies at Cardiff on Thursday.

Tuesday, May 18

HARTY AND MYSELF WERE 40 quid down to Flem and Nath so the euchre on the trip to Cardiff was vital if we didn't want to be taking out a mortgage. After three hours of cards it was all square so our debt didn't move. Still don't trust their body language though.

On the trip we pulled together a bogus Welsh immigration form, and Bully kindly fell for one of the oldest tricks. He filled out the form, produced his passport and officially handed them in, to everyone's amusement. Bully was also the recipient of the first fine on tour – he had forgotten about the dress code and had fronted up to yesterday's game in the wrong tracksuit. A few quid would now find its way into the social fund. Adam is the team fines master, and there's a sense of irony here as Adam is normally the major source of revenue for the social committee. A well thought through appointment by DJ?

On arrival at the Copthorne Hotel in Cardiff, we knocked into the Welsh rugby team, who were departing on a tour to Argentina. A few of the boys yarned with Shane Howarth, and DJ caught up with his old mate Graham Henry, who's a legend around here now after his deeds with their rugby team. There were a few big Welsh boyos around. I don't think that too many cricketers could lock or prop a rugby scrum.

Harty and myself jumped into Waddle's hire car and shot into Cardiff with a view to getting a look at the rebuilt Cardiff Arms Park. The ground seemed nowhere near complete and there were construction workers everywhere. We just walked past them all and ended up deep in the bowels of the new ground. **When we asked some workers for directions, we were quickly told that the public were banned and that everyone needed a hard hat on. We scarpered back to the surface pretty quickly.**

The World Cup merry-go-round has really started now. It's full on and most of the guys turn in for an early night. Before that, though, a few of us sampled a local feed – Welsh pork and leek sausage on mashed spud and covered in brown onion sauce. Great.

GRAND LARSENY

Wednesday, May 19

PRACTICE AT SOPHIA GARDENS, home of Glamorgan CCC and venue of tomorrow's match. The boys practised well and were quite relaxed. No sign of any nerves. **One of the locals noted that we seemed to enjoy our practice, that we trained hard but also had a smile on our faces and that there was a lot of chat.** This, he reported, had been different to the Aussies, who had slogged it out for a couple of hours, with little being said, and in a really structured and disciplined way. There's nothing wrong with that, of course, but I think our practices reflect where we are at with our game. Short and sharp, with fun and variety. The work ethic is also great, with most of the guys putting in extra time on skills that need sharpening up.

Flem asked me to say a few words at his meeting in the evening. I don't usually say a great deal in meetings, preferring to chat more with the guys when I'm one-on-one. Also, we have quite a few guys who enjoy talking at our meetings. I told the guys that over the last four games we hadn't really been placed under any sustained pressure. I said we had to expect it from the Aussies, and be ready to confront it and absorb it, and to deal with it in whatever way was our individual style. I mentioned that I sensed something special, and that if we achieved what no-one over here thought was possible – a win – then the snowball would really start rolling. I left the guys with a few words I'd seen on a car ad on TV. It finished with: STAND *and* FIGHT *or* RUN *and* FALL. It was up to the guys what way they wanted to go. The selectors named the same playing XI that beat Bangladesh.

That evening I met up with Alan Isaac of Wellington, a New Zealand Cricket board member, and a guy I really respect. Zak is top man at KPMG, has been a selector for the Wellington team, played years of senior cricket, and helped me as a youngster at Johnsonville CC. **He was pretty gutted when I ended up at Onslow and we still share a laugh about Onslow poaching me.** It's a bit ironic that my son Corey has just started playing cricket and rugby for the blue-and-blue of Johnsonville. We had a good yarn about a number of things and I'm sure I left him in no doubt that we had a game to win tomorrow.

Thursday, May 20

NEW ZEALAND V AUSTRALIA AT GLAMORGAN
Australia	213-8	
New Zealand	214-5	Win by 5 wickets

YES! IT'S SO HARD to put on paper the incredible emotions after beating the old enemy in a match as important as this one. I've never had a feeling like it in all my years of cricket. When Twosey hit the winning four over mid-on off Damien Fleming's bowling, the changing room just erupted. **The boys were all hugging each other and jumping around screaming like madmen. I'll never forget the look on DJ's face. He was so rapt and proud, and Stumper was just pumped.** You've got to be thrilled for the coach. Being an Aussie, this must have been a small dream come true for him. The Kiwi supporters, who out-yelled the Aussie supporters all day, flocked under our changing room and were chanting and doing hakas. They were just brilliant all day, and I know they had a day they'll never forget. Normally champagne is reserved for winning cups or championships. However we thought today deserved a small celebration, so we popped open the magnum I had won for my Man of the Match against Bangladesh and toasted each other.

It was just fantastic, made even better by seeing the looks on the Aussies' faces! They were shattered and gutted. A couple of our guys popped into their changing room to swap shirts about half an hour after the end and said that it was like a morgue. They're a great team who play the game in a hard fashion, and to knock them over in a World Cup (as we did in 1992) is something pretty special. **Graham Henry also popped into the changing room with a huge smile on his face and offered his congratulations.**

We played the game in a really controlled way. Twice we got out of tight spots, once when Ponting and Lehmann were developing a partnership, and then when we were 49-4 chasing their total. Both times we showed great fight and commitment to turn the tables. GA was brilliant with the ball again, and the bowling and fielding generally was top drawer. Then Cairnsy and Twosey turned it on with the bat in a superb match-winning partnership.

The behaviour of the players inside the changing room and the viewing room is always interesting. Some guys have the ability to sit quietly and take in every ball in a controlled manner, no matter what the situation in the middle. **Others pace the changing room, trying to control their nervous energy. Some talk – Harry's definitely in that category.** Others have their bat in hand, practising shots, putting on and taking off their gloves, checking the sprigs in their boots are tight enough – anything to distract themselves from what is happening in the middle.

Raz and GA after our victory over Australia.

GA got into the habit of establishing a 'quiet area', usually Fran's physio room, which became a retreat for whoever wanted a few minutes away from the tension. This was by invitation only, with Harry never a guest. **Another classic retreat is the toilet, and I must admit I fall into this category.** Usually I'd knock into the same guys in this room and after about your third visit you actually found it was a pointless trip other than wasting another five minutes. Always fun trying to guess who was in the cubicle next to you, though. I suppose I'm a pacer. I find it hard to stay put for a period of time and tend to do a number of things over the duration of the innings in an effort to keep the mind relaxed. The main aim, of course, is to relax, and not let the tension overwhelm you. And as a unit, you must stay positive and 'as one' through the good times and the bad. There's nothing worse than a guy with bad body language, and you learn very quickly to ensure that you keep the negative or critical thoughts bottled up.

I rang Karen and my parents straight away to share the moment and they were all thrilled, but suffering through lack of sleep. It's fair to say that it was a pretty stoked group of cricketers who shared a few beers back in the hotel bar.

Friday, May 21

WOKE UP AND PINCHED myself to make sure yesterday had actually happened. We were brought back to reality quickly with a recovery swim followed by a debrief of the match. As usual, Bert and Stumper made sure we left the meeting with our feet firmly planted on the ground, with our thoughts now switched to the upcoming Windies match.

We have a small tradition that takes place from time to time at our debrief meeting. **We have what has been labelled the 'BTB Club', and to gain admittance to the club you have to be deemed to be showing day-in-day out loyalty to all of our values.** Shotty determines who receives their card, and a good point is that if a player feels he has let himself or the team down in terms of the values, he has the option of returning his card. I was lucky enough to receive my card at today's meeting, and I saw it as a small reinforcement that I haven't been letting any of my own standards slip. As Bert and Stumper stress to us all, 'If you trust both your own and the team's systems and processes, and continue to trust them through good times and bad, then you'll eventually come out on the right side of the ledger.' Great advice I reckon, and not only for cricketers, either.

The bus trip to Southampton was a shocker, only because Harty and I were another 40 quid down to Fleming and Astle. We will work out their system! The pile of congratulation faxes passed around the bus was huge. They came from everywhere and everyone, schools in NZ, companies, individuals, politicians, sporting organisations, and family and friends. It's great to feel all the support out there.

Saturday, May 22

AFTER TRAINING WE WERE invited down to a local bar, *Walkabout*, set up with an Aussie and Kiwi theme. The manager was an ex-Kiwi, who was rapt to have us in. He kindly fronted for lunch and the cokes and lemonades. **The main reason for being there, though, was to watch the Crusaders v Reds Super 12 semi-final on the big screen.** The Cantabs (Messrs Fleming, Astle, Allott, Cairns, and McMillan) can be a painful and parochial lot. They were more animated and vocal than normal today, and that's saying something. Even Bully came out of the closet as a red-and-black supporter, wearing a Crusaders beanie, although at one stage he biffed it in the corner as they fell behind on the scoreboard. It was great to be Kiwi, though, as the Crusaders came through, showing some good old-fashioned guts and determination. Something we can take into Monday's match maybe.

A few of us then eased back at the hotel to watch the FA Cup final between Newcastle and that red team from Manchester. We had made ourselves comfortable in the lounge bar, a few of us ordered coffees and Bert asked for a pot of tea as he wanted to use his very special big mug that he carries around with him. **No dramas, until the young waiter presented Bert with a bill for 10 quid. That's $NZ30, or as we pointed out, $15 a tea-bag.** Now Bert is a pretty gentle sort of guy. He's not called Smiley because of his nasty streak, that's for sure. However, we were privileged today to see his other side. The four-letter word even slipped out of his mouth at one stage, and the ashen-faced young waiter sped back to the kitchen with his tail between his legs. Out came the female supervisor with her prepared speech, saying that the pot actually held five cups of tea, and as a cup was £2.25p (damned expensive anyway) he was, in fact, getting it cheap! Well, that was the last straw. He sent her on her bike and hunted down the Duty Manager. He had the others in the bar, who were watching the footie, listening in, nodding and laughing. He struck a compromise of £5 with the boss, and the long and short of it was that when he went to pay his bill afterwards there was actually no charge at all. Great pantomime it was. For the record, the red team beat Newcastle 2-0 to secure the second leg of their potential treble.

Later, the Stunned Mullets had an afternoon of sailing off the Southampton coast. They were guests on one of the Round-the-World yachts, and all came back windblown and totally fizzing. **Nashy in his own mad way climbed the mast, Flem, as one would expect, took the wheel, and Adam refused to do any of the grinding.** On the Sky World Cup programme that night, the sailors were featured looking splendid in their silver jackets and sunglasses. The Eels, though, were gutted to find that Stumper (an Eels member) had wangled an invite, and to make matters worse actually said on camera that he enjoyed the Mullets' company and was impressed with them as a team. Dan Vettori, the Eels captain, was almost sick and promptly suspended the coach from any Eels events until further notice. Turncoat, traitor, a knife in the back from the coach. We Eels weren't happy.

The South Africans have quickly established themselves as the hot favourites for the World Cup. They demolished England by 122 runs today, and have been playing like a team who expect to win. Their top and middle-order batting has been a little reckless, but their depth is amazing and probably allows this approach. A guy like Klusener can cruise in at No 9 and smack it around. It's their bowling that is so impressive. They are demanding with their line and length, and are at you all day. Of course, they're backed up by a great fielding unit, led by the one and only Jonty Rhodes. **What I find inspiring about the South Africans is their professional attitude off the park. They leave no stone unturned in terms of preparation, and the driving force is definitely Hansie Cronje.** I remember dropping into his hotel room when we played South Africa in the 1996 World Cup in Faisalabad, and my eyes nearly popped out. It resembled a War Room, with laptop, printer, TV and video player, along with what seemed like hundreds of video tapes, whiteboard and flipchart, fax and mobile phone. There was also a bed in there somewhere. It summed up his approach to his cricket: total preparation. Alvin Kallicharran, the Kenyan coach, was quoted in a newspaper over here saying, 'Gone are the days when you can just turn up and perhaps even cause an upset. Teams like South Africa are just too good to be caught out.' Spot on, Alvin. My feeling is that to beat this team, of course you have to score more runs than them on the park, but you also must 'out-prepare' them off it.

On this note, one tool that we are now using which enables us to prepare more thoroughly is a video analysis computer, which has been affectionately named Pooch by Ashley Ross, whose baby it is. NZC invested in Pooch, through the New Zealand Sports Foundation, at the start of last season and it's a very handy tool, not only for analysing your own game, but for closely examining the opposition players. **It's the old story - often you've got no idea that you're slipping up technically until you see it on video.** Pooch receives a direct feed from the TV control van on the ground, and the 'driver' (usually Shotty) then makes on-the-spot decisions about line and length if we're bowling, or decision-making and execution if batting, and feeds them into Pooch. This then enables me, as a bowler, to sit down the next day with Stumper or Shotty, and look at a condensed form of the 60 balls I bowled and to analyse my performance. **Against South Africa in the recent home series, it became apparent that Harry, Dan, and myself were being particularly targeted by the South Africans when we came on to bowl.** I used Pooch and along with Shotty had a good look at the likes of Kirsten, Cronje and Kallis, who seemed to be the guys willing to come down the wicket to me. We looked for themes and patterns in what balls they came down on. For instance, we often found they had a sighter on the first ball of an over, then came down on the second ball. We had a look at their pre-delivery movements and found Kirsten had a standard 'back and across' movement. However, when he looked to charge me his first movement was onto the front foot. Shotty and I decided that if I caught the movement quickly enough I would bowl shorter and faster and look for a stumping or nick. Well, wouldn't you believe it – the following day at the Basin Reserve it worked beautifully. Kirsten stumped Parore, bowled Larsen! Ten out of ten for preparation and one up for the Pooch.

Sunday, May 23

Bully, Harty, Dan and Doully all headed off for games of cricket with local Hampshire Sunday teams. They obviously hadn't had much cricket over the last week or so, so it was a good chance for them to get in some match practice, even if the standard wasn't crash hot. **Harty related that his team had a rousing team talk, saying it was a big match and that their opposition was pretty useful.** He said the game turned out to be about fourth-grade standard. Doully came back sporting a huge bruise on his arm, courtesy of an ill-directed beamer from an enthusiastic opening bowler. And Bully, who was looking

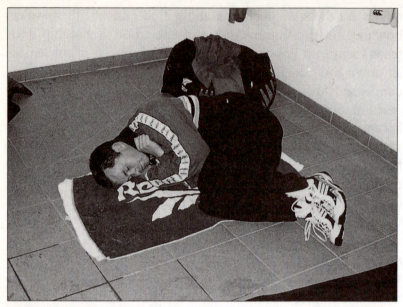

If you want to track the Dirties down, check out the showers. Harty takes a nap.

forward to 'bowling real fast and sticking it up a few of the locals', bowled four overs of gentle medium pace. He reckons he would have killed someone if he had wound up the speed.

The playing XI for tomorrow has already been named. We have made no changes. We had a final shakedown at the Hampshire county ground. Again I felt that we trained well, although I sense a bit of an emotional 'hangover' after the Aussie win. The pitch looks OK. However **I'm sure it will nip around a little most of the day. Just hope Flem has the birdie on his shoulder with the toss.** It's just so critical for us all to lift ourselves again for what is going to be a huge game against a fired-up Windies team, who are desperate for a good performance. We know we will be under the microscope at home, as one of the big criticisms of the team in recent years has been our inability to front up on a consistent basis. We acknowledge that is a fact, and we talk about it often in our meetings. To me it's all about being more ruthless and hard-nosed as individuals.

LET THE GAMES BEGIN

Monday, May 24

NEW ZEALAND V WEST INDIES AT SOUTHAMPTON
New Zealand   156 all out
West Indies   160-3   Loss by 7 wickets

UNDONE BY A BETTER team on the day. The toss again proved important. In fact, you could say it was crucial. Lara certainly didn't hesitate in bowling first. **Ambrose and Walsh didn't give us a look in. Both were pretty fired up, and you can't get two more seasoned campaigners to give the new ball to in conditions that suit them.** They share 71 years of experience for starters. They have 340 ODIs between them, 400 wickets and an average economy rate of 3.7 runs an over. Useful stats! They bowled a great line and length, getting good bounce and movement, and the free-scoring Nath, Macca, and Flem just didn't have any opportunities to free their arms. At 80-odd for seven, it was a long way back. We fought pretty well down the order, and then again in the field, but all in a lost cause, really.

I bowled my first four overs for four runs, then Lara decided it was time. The little medium-pacer had to go. He smacked a huge six back over my head, then a big inside-out four over extra cover. Jacobs nicked me for four, and, along with a single a ball, my last three overs went for 25. **Bowling to the special players like Lara, Tendulkar, Mark Waugh and Aravinda – you always get the feeling that they have that extra bit of class and that extra bit of time to play their shots.** Good balls get worked around the park with ease for ones and twos, and they have the big shots as well. Brian showed me a couple of those today.

Back at the hotel, DJ asked me to do an interview on *Radio Sport* with Andrew Dewhurst. It was pretty standard stuff, and I talked about the influence of the toss, the seaming wicket and the overhead conditions, a few loose shots from the batsmen, and the spirit I thought we showed bowling and fielding. However, this seemed to fall on deaf ears with Andrew. He asked me if I thought that New Zealand had

Walsh and Ambrose... deadly on a seaming wicket.

shown their perennial weakness in this game – when we came up against a top team and the going got tough (Ambrose and Walsh on a seaming, bouncing wicket), was the application missing? I was dumbfounded and had to catch my breath before I replied. I reiterated how important I thought the toss had been, stressing the quality of the bowling, and said that the feeling within the team was as good as I'd seen. **The damage had been done, however, as Andrew had sown that negative seed into the minds of his listeners.** My reply didn't matter whatsoever. It seemed remarkable to me that only three days ago we had had a really famous victory, showing *huge* amounts of application, and already this application was being questioned by the media. How fickle life can be.

Talking about the media, I've always had a pretty good relationship with those people who have so much power in shaping public opinion in this country. I've had a fair run from the media, and there are only a couple of New Zealand journos that I won't give my all to. These guys I think regularly sensationalise and are at all times looking for the controversial angle. If I was to sum up how I think the New Zealand cricket media operates, then I'd put it this way. In every situation, there is usually good and bad, obviously in varying degrees. My feeling is that our media will focus primarily on the bad, the negative. If there was a choice between a positive or a negative headline, I know which one would usually be pulled out by the sub-editor. However, what it means from the players' perspective is that we learn pretty damned quickly to sit on the fence, to be neutral, and to produce the 'politically correct' answers. The trust isn't always there, and subsequently all the old worn cliches emerge, often at the expense of the flair of the individual player. **The bottom line for me is that players want balance and objectivity from the media, which I don't think is always the case.** I will add a wee rider here: boy, I'd hate to be an English cricketer.

Tuesday, May 25

THE MIDLAND HOTEL IN Derby is our next residence. Not crash hot. No gym, no swimming pool, and no Sky TV (which means no watching World Cup cricket). The £44 room tariff compared to the £100-plus at our other venues, sums it up I suppose.

On the way to Derby, the boys involved in the card schools at the back of the bus started making accusations about some bad smells that were wafting around. No-one was spared. However, everyone denied that the smells had emanated from them. Team protocol says that one owns up if guilty, so it appeared we had a liar among us. However, minutes later Hornet emerged from the bus toilet, a satisfied look on his face. He took a major ribbing from the boys, who still had t-shirts pulled up over their faces. A new travelling rule was quickly passed.

Our loss yesterday makes our group position really interesting. If we beat Pakistan we qualify and, most importantly, take four points through to the Super Six if Aussie also qualify. If we don't win and beat Scotland in our last match then there is the possibility that it'll come down to run rates. On that note, it was crucial yesterday that we managed to squeeze out 45 overs before the Windies knocked off the small target. And the Aussie v Windies match is looming as the big one. If the Aussies lose, they're on their way home, and there wouldn't have been too many who would have forecast that. From our perspective, we want the Aussies to qualify for obvious reasons.

Another checkpoint from Bert, who insisted at our debrief that everyone have a close and honest look at themselves, to check out their personal disciplines, to make sure our off-the-park preparation was as thorough as possible. He then added a new item to the treasure chest. He threw in a pin, calling it a 'Discipin', and said that it was to be used to prick and prod people when they might be inadvertently heading off the track. A not-so-subtle reminder for the boys. **Stumper confirmed what we all knew, that we'd had a hiccup, that there were contributing factors to the loss.** He also stressed the importance of the next three days in terms of our preparation for Pakistan.

Rang home and got an update from my nine-year-old daughter, Nadia, as Karen was out grocery shopping (I hope there was a baby-sitter there somewhere). Corey had scored three tries in his rugby and had been on a school trip to the zoo, and Vanessa, my three-year-old, had been out to a wee friend's birthday party. Nadia had lost her netball, indoor cricket and water polo (oh dear, a bad day), but said she'd enjoyed herself. She'll learn. She also said that Mum had just bought a new $600 vacuum cleaner. **There's one thing for sure, while I'm away doing what I love on the other side of the world, the domestic duties at home don't disappear.** Nadia's pretty rapt because she's allowed to sleep in Mum's bed on Friday night and watch the Pakistan match on Sky TV. So, while the World Cup carnival continues here in England, life goes on in Paparangi, Wellington.

Wednesday, May 26

TODAY WE WATCHED TWO of the best innings to date in the World Cup. Dravid and Ganguly have just scored huge centuries and had the Sri Lankan bowlers totally at their mercy. They racked up the largest partnership in ODIs and India the second highest ODI score of 373-6. Not surprisingly, the wicket at Taunton was probably the best batting deck seen yet in the comp (about bloody time, I hear the batters say). I feel they're a team that has been a bit under-rated, with real class batsmen. And also Tendulkar is now dedicating this tournament to his late father. Danger!

The Hart Throbs had a morning out at Alton Towers, a huge fun park about 45 minutes out of Derby. **Harry went mad (no surprise there), going on every thrill-seeking ride possible, and Bully also got his full 17 quids' worth.** The Throbs have had some internal strife, so obviously today was an effort to get some bonding going.

First injury scares with Nashy and Twosey taking only a small part in our late afternoon practice at The Racecourse, home of Derbyshire CCC. Both have minor leg problems and we're hopeful they'll be OK for Friday. We've done well to this point with no injuries to speak. Touch wood things remain that way.

We've suffered badly with injuries in the past, particularly to the bowlers. In the last year there has been a reduction in the number of these injuries. A real effort by the New Zealand management team to reduce and manage the overall workload of bowlers has been the major factor, in my opinion. **It was probably only three years ago that the boys had affectionately nicknamed me the 'bowling machine'. This was due to the number of overs I bowled at practice.** I would be thrown the ball in one net, would normally have to truck through 10 or so overs – a good hour of bowling, and then that was job complete. You didn't even consider telling the coach that you'd had enough. It was just expected. Even the day before a match, I was expected to bowl enough to keep the batsmen happy. One occasion will remain with me forever. In 1997 we were in Bulawayo for the second test against Zimbabwe, and the day before the test we had an open wicket practice in about 30-degree heat. It lasted for three hours. Our opening bowlers for the test were Shayne O'Connor and David Sewell, who bowled about ten overs each. They were both knackered. Well, surprise, surprise, they were a little short of a gallop the next day and both took a bit of stick from the Zim batsmen, and Sewelly never played again.

Now things are structured and controlled in a much tighter fashion. Obviously early in the season you need to get overs under the belt, to get your rhythm and technique right. **But once the season is under way, 30 quality deliveries is considered a maximum number for the medium and quick bowlers. Five overs only.** One of the management team will be counting deliveries and will count down the last over or so. And from Fran's standpoint, he's always there wearing his physio hat, making sure the ball is out of our hand after the five overs. We play so much now that this change was crucial. What it means is that the onus falls on Stumper to make sure that quality net bowlers are available so our batsmen don't miss out. I know from my perspective that once I'm in rhythm and the ball is coming out OK, I need only the five overs to top up on my stock deliveries, and to work on variations, such as the slower ball or yorker.

There are other major factors that have assisted us in injury prevention. Ashley Ross, and his biomechanical work with the bowlers, has been excellent. His work with the younger guys coming through will have flow-through effects. **His aim is to help the bowlers become more efficient in their actions and to eliminate anything that could be causing unwanted stress on the body.**

Generally the boys are probably more aware of their own bodies, what they need personally in terms of fitness requirements, and are more conscious of the rest and down time that is needed to let the body recover. Massage has also been a key for me. Before this tournament, the management team established a network of masseurs around England, and at any time they are on-call to come in and work with the boys. Twosey, Nashy, Cairnsy, and myself are the guys who take full advantage of this. One guy who came and worked with us in Cardiff was brilliant, the best massage I've ever had. He had

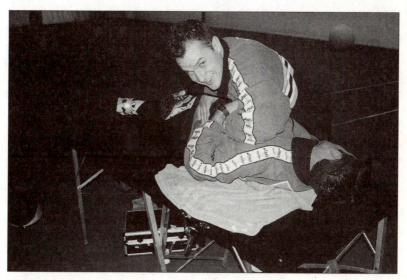

Mark Harrison gets down to work on Nath.

represented England at gymnastics and really knew what was required. He had also worked with the Aussie bowlers and made an interesting comment about the bad state of their quick bowlers' bodies. **My response was pretty quick to him: 'They may have bad bodies, but don't worry about the Aussies, they've always got what it takes up top.'**

The whole squad strolled down to a local sports and leisure centre for dinner and to watch the European Champions Trophy final between Manchester Utd and Bayern Munich. Bayern Munich scored early and United then couldn't break down their defence. With time up, United quite amazingly scored twice within a minute to grab the win. It was an almost unbelievable finish, and the scenes at the end summed up to me what playing elite sport is all about. The emotions were dramatic, at both ends of the scale. The stakes at the top level are so high, with losers suffering utter despair and the winners total euphoria. We play to win, for ourselves and our country, and to hopefully enjoy that euphoria. Who wouldn't want to be one of the United players on this night? Or hold the World Cup of cricket in about four weeks' time?

Thursday, May 27

THE LOWER ORDER BATSMEN (Larsen and Allott) and the four non-players (Doull, Hart, Vettori, Bulfin) hit the nets at 9am, an hour earlier than the rest of the boys. It was our chance for a good bat against the Derbyshire 2nd XI bowlers. **However, Stumper took it as an opportunity to totally destroy my batting confidence on a slow turner, his off-spinners having me in trouble every ball, culminating in him taking a smart caught and bowled. He loved it.** He often bowls when we're short of bowlers and takes particular joy in getting Flem and Twosey out.

Nets always have a competitive edge, the bowlers hate getting whacked, and vice versa, the batsmen enjoy getting on top of the bowlers. Practice is always a great place to make a statement to the selectors, and one guy who's really busted his gut here is Bully. He's bowled really quick at times, and on occasions the skipper has even had to tell him to pitch it up a little more. **He likes seeing the batsmen ducking and weaving for sure, and I've had to keep telling him that I'm a fellow Wellingtonian and 36 years old.** He hit Harty in the chest at The Oval and Harty went down like a sack of spuds. The tough ND man got straight up, but his heavy breathing and white face gave him away. And on the morning – yes, the morning – of the Aussie match, Bully bounced Cairnsy in the nets and smashed him on the arm. You can't doubt the effort, but common sense deserted him on this one.

At our team meeting, Flem outlined a pretty major change to the batting order if we were to bat first in the match. As a result of the swinging ball, the seaming wickets, and the poor starts we had been experiencing, Flem and Stumper have decided to approach the first eight overs of the innings in 'test match' mode. In other words, preservation of wickets and careful selection of shots. **Hornet, Twosey and Adam were deemed to have the best techniques to achieve this and they would bat Nos 1, 2 and 3, with Nath, Flem and Macca (the strokemakers) to bat after that.** The concept is fine and I admire Flem for implementing change quickly in an attempt to aid the team cause. I have a suspicion, though, that part of the aim is to protect Nath from the new ball as he is having a bit of a nightmare trot. I wonder if he had scored a couple of 30s whether the change would have been made. Also, I feel a bit for Twosey who at this point has really cemented a middle-order spot, and offers us reliability through the middle stages. If we get through the first eight overs, the danger period when the ball swings most, then Adam drops back down to his normal spot at seven. And if we bat second, then the order is determined at the break, based on the match situation.

Tomorrow is a huge game for us in the context of the whole tournament. We know we need to hit the road at full speed. Anything less and the Pakistanis will hit us hard. As a team they have come to the boil at the right time. They are emotional, hugely talented and full of flair. They have injected youth into their team, and **Wasim Akram always holds the reins. After 10 years of playing international cricket, I'm in no doubt that Akram is the greatest all-round cricketer I've come up against.** He is inspirational to his team. In the past they have had rifts and factions, and obvious in-fighting. However, at the moment they appear a tight unit, a direct reflection on Akram's captaincy. I've found that at times their emotions can be their weakness, and you can look to exploit this. We need to get on top of them early, and then not let go for a better grab. We must attempt to maintain pressure on them throughout. If you let them take the initiative, it's extremely hard to wrest it back.

Friday, May 28

NEW ZEALAND V PAKISTAN AT DERBY
Pakistan   269-8
New Zealand   207-8   Loss by 62 runs

I HIT MY ROOM early tonight. Normally after a match, win or lose, I like to head out with the guys and have a few quiet ones. It helps to unwind and digest the game with the boys. Tonight my heart was just not in it. The match today was huge for us, as a win would have seen us odds-on for a semi-final spot. To not compete on the day, and to see the difference between the teams was pretty distressing. **We were outplayed from ball one, when Nashy was smashed through mid-wicket by Anwar for four.** They got a flyer, 47 off the first six overs, which you just can't afford on these wickets. I got as frustrated as I ever have with my bowling. My job is obviously to go for as few runs as possible off my 10 overs and if I can sneak one or two wickets, that's a bonus. The aim is not to get hit for boundaries, and to force the batsmen to look for singles only. I went for 35, which is OK. However, I never felt in control. Ijaz the Axeman (he wields the bat like an axe) played me really well. When I got too straight he turned me through square for one, and when I readjusted my line to just outside off stump, he opened the face, working me down to third man. When I tried pitching it up a bit, he rocked forward and knocked it into the gap at cover or squeezed it down to fine leg. **The Asian players can be frustrating to bowl to. They are extremely wristy and are more unorthodox in their working of the ball than their English, Aussie, and South African counterparts,** who tend to play more orthodox cricket shots and use the full face of the bat more.

GA went for 64 off his 10, although he did take four wickets, and BA went for 47 off 7. It's hard to pull it back when two of the front-liners go for around seven an over. The boundary on one side was huge, MCG-like, and very hard to protect. There was acres of space and the Pakistanis seemed to knock it into the gaps regularly. With a few overs to go and after a couple of long lumbering runs after the ball from yours truly, Nashy replaced me out in the deep and I completed the innings in the inner circle. I had been red-carded by the skipper. I think he felt that the speed and athleticism of Nash was probably a slightly better option than the 36-year-old limbs of Larsen.

Making 270 was going to be a huge ask against that attack and it wasn't an overly bubbly group of guys who sat down to lunch. As an aside, playing the Asian countries is great as curry is always on the lunch menu. Today we had a sweet chicken curry, rice and poppadoms. Fantastic.

The order reverted back to normal and normal was also the type of start we had: bad! **We've got a major problem on our hands with Hornet and Nath's form. Neither has got a run yet and we've been two or three for spit (as we say) in every innings.** It puts too much pressure on the middle-order to have to front every time. The complicating factor is that our four non-players are all bowlers, which I suppose brings attention to the overall balance of our squad of 15. In the middle of the innings Cairnsy and Adam came and went quickly with ducks, and it was all over. With the result basically confirmed (we needed about 10 an over for the last 15 overs and were seven down), we had the

I won't be scoring a hundred today... New Zealand v Pakistan at Derby.

embarrassing job of having to bat out the overs in order to assist our net run rate. This we achieved OK, but it didn't make pretty watching. All in all a crap day – cold, windy, a poor ground (the Derby county ground is set in the middle of an old racecourse), and average facilities, matched by our performance.

LET THE GAMES BEGIN

Fanatical, passionate, emotional... the Pakistani supporters.

Saturday, May 29

DRIFTED INTO DERBY WITH Hornet, with the thought of getting a few presents on board for Karen and the kids. As usual, I looked at plenty, and bought little apart from for myself. That won't surprise Karen. **It must be a male thing to leave everything until the last minute, and I certainly do that well.** Nadia has the only present to date, and I actually bought that for myself. I picked up a stereo in Singapore on the way over. Cart it around for using in my hotel room and have had the inspiring thought of giving it to Nards when I get home. With a few *Spice Girls* and *Back Street Boys* CDs, I'll be the best Dad around.

Zimbabwe have turned Group A upside down by beating South Africa today. A few of the boys met up in a local to watch the end of the game (no Sky in the hotel), and the unthinkable is starting to pan out. With the Zimbos winning and England off for rain and in trouble against India, the possibility exists that England may not qualify for the next stage. Wouldn't that get the tabloid writers humming! There's one thing for sure: the Poms will be having a very nervous night's sleep tonight.

Sunday, May 30

BEFORE HEADING TO EDINBURGH, we watched the Highlanders v Crusaders Super 12 final that had been taped for us. Unfortunately, we once more had the Cantab contingent gloating and ho-humming about how great it is to wear the red-and-black and what a marvellous feeling winning is. **They even pulled out the 'Hurricanes' chant for Twosey's and my benefit. Provincial rivalry while on tour? You bet!** Macca had a bit of a windfall on the result. He had thrown $20 on the Crusaders when they had drifted out to 25/1 after the bad start to their campaign. To say he was smiling was an understatement. We were all rapt for Bert, who performs the same role for the Crusaders as he does for us. He was absolutely stoked, but Gilbert Enoka being Gilbert Enoka, he quickly told us that a win tomorrow against Scotland would make him just as happy. There's one thing about Smiley Spice – if you ever see him without a smile on his dial you know something is wrong.

We bused it up to Birmingham, where we caught a lunchtime flight to Edinburgh. **I must admit I've become quite caught up in the Manchester United success, in terms of what makes them tick and how they go about things.** There's so much sports people can learn by studying outfits like United, because, let's face it, we'd all love to be in their shoes at the moment. I was reading the paper on the plane and saw a quote from Alex Ferguson, their manager. Asked to put a finger on the reason for their success, he simply said, 'Some people like to go to Blackpool for their holiday, others want to go to the moon.' Tomorrow is going to be a true test for the New Zealand cricket team along these lines. How much do we really want to progress to the next stage of the World Cup?

LET THE GAMES BEGIN

Today was a huge one in sorting out the two groups. **The first shock involved the hosts. The England boys are now scarpering back home with their tails between their legs a little sooner than they thought.** India duly took the last seven England wickets to book their spot in the Super Six and that condemned England to fourth spot on run rates in Group A. I'm sure the Poms didn't think that they'd be playing Sunday League cricket for their counties this weekend. On a personal note I'm a bit disappointed that England are out, as the tournament will not quite be the same from a local hype point of view with the host team gone. Their batting let them down badly in two crucial games, and there's a real message there for us. As for their bowlers, I thought Mullally was superb throughout, Goughy never stopped trying and they had good backup. All to no avail, though.

The other huge game was the Aussie v Windies game at Edgbaston. Glenn McGrath got the new ball back in his hand after bowling first change in the first four matches and made his own statement by taking five wickets and helping to bowl out the Windies for a paltry 110. **We've always been of the opinion that the Windies do well when Lara does well, and today was no exception.** McGrath bowled him with an absolute snorter, a ball that was quick, seamed, and took his off bail. And that delivery in effect ended the match. The Aussies got a flyer, and were heading towards an early shower when things got interesting. They basically blocked out the last 15 overs or so of their innings in an effort to keep the Windies run rate high enough to make our task against Scotland as impossible as they could. They desperately wanted the Windies to qualify and us eliminated so they could carry two points through to the Super Six. We were livid as we watched the Windies lob down over after over of maidens and our task got harder and harder. As professional sportsmen they had to do everything within the rules of the competition to enable their country the best chance of success. If that meant dicking their neighbours then so be it. ANZAC spirit? Pig's ass!

Of course, we're not happy. Gutted is probably closer to the mark. I couldn't even watch it as Steve Waugh and Michael Bevan practised their defensive techniques, and I flicked the TV over to motor racing on another channel. At the end, we were left with the following situation: if we bat first we need to score 275 and then bowl Scotland out for 140. If we bowl first we need to bowl Scotland out for 150 and then knock the runs off in 20 overs. Stiff tasks whatever way you look at it. **I tell you what, there would be no better feeling if we get through tomorrow. It would then be the full middle finger to our near neighbours for all their help.**

When the skipper hunts you down prior to the captain's meeting, it usually means bad news. And this evening he hunted me down. The selectors, Stumper, Flem, and Nashy, have decided to drop me and put Bully in for the extra firepower they think we need to bowl Scotland out cheaply. Being dropped is the worst possible feeling. It's like having your guts ripped out. What made this news even worse was that I hadn't expected it. I thought I had been bowling consistently well and as at today I've got the fifth best economy rate in the cup. Also, after winning the Man of the Match award against Bangladesh, I was really looking forward to playing the other lesser nation on a wicket that looked like it might seam a little. **To top it all off, and not wanting to be too negative, this is potentially my last World Cup game, given our dicey run-rate situation. To have a lasting memory of being dropped for my last game wouldn't be a great feeling.**

The evening was all quite rushed. We had the need to see the end of the Aussie/Windies game, to then calculate run-rates, to re-schedule our team meeting, and for the selectors to pick our Scotland team. All this had to be crammed into a half-hour period for some reason, and let's not forget that these were crucial decisions and our World Cup future was at stake. Along with a few others, I got left with the feeling that hasty decisions were made. A lack of preparedness in our planning left us vulnerable. Campaigns can be won and lost on such small things.

Of course, my fingers are crossed that the boys achieve the special result that is needed tomorrow, that we progress to the Super Six, and that I then get an opportunity to force my way back into the team. I just so much wanted to be a part of tomorrow. What I can't reconcile in my mind is the reasoning behind the change. I know it's about more firepower. We do, however, have three attacking bowlers in Allott, Nash, and Cairns and by keeping it tight at one end (and hopefully taking wickets as well) this generates another type of pressure. Also, if the selectors wanted more firepower, what about Simon Doull, the No 8 test bowler in the world and a great opening swing bowler? He could have opened the bowling with Allott, with Nash, who hasn't picked up many wickets with the new ball, dropping down to first change. **And where in all this does experience fit in a match of such importance? If I sound grumpy, I am.**

It took ages to get to sleep last night. I was stewing over my dropping, and trying to find some – any – positives in it. I was urging myself not to appear negative to the other boys, and made a promise to myself not to sulk about it and to give it heaps the following morning at warm-ups. As a senior player, I didn't want any of the younger guys looking at me and thinking 'selfish sod' and diverting their attention away from the task in hand. My last thought before I nodded off was that I could be on a plane home to New Zealand in two days' time.

Monday, May 31

NEW ZEALAND V SCOTLAND AT EDINBURGH
Scotland 120 all out
New Zealand 121-4 Win by 6 wickets

BRILLIANT. JUST BLOODY BRILLIANT. The boys pulled the big one out of the bag when it was needed. The vital toss was won by Flem and we stuck the Scotties in as per the plan. Three early wickets gave us a great start, but the nerves kicked

Television duties at Edinburgh Castle.

in when they developed a small partnership and eased their way to 60-3. Crossroads time. When I took the drinks out at the first break there were a couple of whispers to me along the lines of, 'I hope these changes don't backfire in our face'.

Every captain will admit that it's nice to have the birdie on the shoulder, and today Flem had it with his bowling changes. We took vital wickets immediately following bowling changes, something that always warms a captain's heart. **Harry cleaned up the tail in his own unique way and we had half the job done. There was no emotion in the shed at the break, just a steely resolve now that we were extremely close to nailing our stage-one goal.** I must admit to thinking about the Aussie and West Indian players, who would have been sitting in their hotels watching our effort. I hope they had a big sweat on.

We had 21 overs in which to knock off the runs and qualify on run rate. Hornet had also been dropped for this match and Matthew Hart came in, and, a little surprisingly to some, was asked to open the innings. Unfortunately, Harty got bowled second ball, then Nath nicked out again and we were in the familiar position of 20-2. Back came the nerves. Twosey was the man, however, enjoying some luck in between some big clean hitting and he and Cairnsy saw us through, big BA smacking a ball out of the park to win the game. We needed only 17 overs and had knocked the runs off in a really clinical way. **It was a happy bunch of guys at the end. Not the uncontrolled euphoria of the Aussie win (which to me just couldn't be bettered), but a real warm feeling tempered with the fact that the hard work was just starting. The word 'Australia' was also mentioned a few times, not always in glowing terms, either.**

The support here again was superb, there were Kiwis coming out of the woodwork all round Britain. It's a special feeling to see the New Zealand flags flying, the black and white painted faces and, of course, the compulsory post-match haka. I think the Kiwis do pretty well on the drinking front, too. After the match we had to walk out of the ground and about a hundred metres down a narrow road that our bus couldn't negotiate. We were out amongst the masses, the majority of whom were Kiwis. They were yelling and screaming, chanting the boys' names, and were just stoked to be close to the players. It took about 10 minutes for the bus to turn up, and what a brilliant 10 minutes it was. The police had to close off the end of the road as the supporters just wouldn't move. **They just wanted to yarn, to shake our hands, and to pat us on the back.** Cairnsy and I were each given a Maori poi by one of the fans, and she tied it to our bag, saying it was our good luck poi for the rest of the tournament. It won't leave my bag. Sometimes we become a little bit insulated to what's happening out on the streets, and it takes moments like this, standing on a street corner in Edinburgh with the grassroots supporters (the punters, as we call them) to give you a good dose of reality.

The bottom line in Group B is that the Windies are out and winging their way back to the Caribbean. They'll be gutted, and rightly so. There was nothing really between the Aussies, the Windies, and ourselves. We all beat each other, and while I like the format of the tournament (easy to say that now, I suppose), it's still a hard school to think that a slightly poorer run rate sends you home from a World Cup tournament that rolls around only every four years. I'm sure England would nod their heads on this one. Still, there are big stakes at this level, and let's not forget that both the Aussies and Windies were all for shafting us a couple of days ago.

Then There Were Six

Tuesday, June 1

FIRST DAY OF THE month, and it made me think of home. Nadia gets me every month with the old 'a pinch and a punch for the first of the month' trick. Mind you, it's usually when I'm lying in bed half asleep.

It's fair to say that most of the guys were feeling a bit seedy this morning. One could say that our recovery session mid-morning in a local gym was less than intense. We celebrated well into the night, and deserved to. For probably the first time since the tournament began, we had time to let the hair down and have a good blowout. **Flem and I shared a beer at one stage and he acknowledged things had been a bit rushed two nights ago and that in hindsight the team selection had not been thought through enough, and a couple of mistakes had been made.** He mentioned that in future if he encountered similar situations he would insist on naming a squad, not a playing XI, and sleep on things before making a final decision in the morning. Good common sense. I remember dancing at one stage with Chris and Linda Harris – a sorry sight that would be, with my two left feet. Also I woke with a sore left nipple, and vaguely remembered Nashy trying to rip it off at some point. He gets quite fired up when in party mode and has a great time. Martin Leslie (Scotland flanker and a good Wellington man) was also

Arise, Sir Harry. GA does the honours at Edinburgh Castle.

out having a beer with us and took Nashy's wrath at one stage, something along the lines of, 'Shit, you're not as big as I thought you were. I think I could take you!'

We don't play until Sunday and the Super Six draw has us playing Zimbabwe first at Headingley. We travel to London tomorrow for a World Cup function (to meet the Queen), then head to Leeds on Thursday, where it's back into practice and preparation.

The day off gives us a chance to put the tourist hat on and head off to Edinburgh Castle. GA, Harry and Linda, Harty, Pete (the Pooch operator) and I spent an enjoyable couple of hours wandering around what is a fantastic Scottish landmark. The Castle is intriguing and I certainly felt naive and ignorant of Scottish history as our guide led us around the old fortress. The place is just huge, and it wasn't too hard to visualise the past and some of the attacks that have taken place on the Castle over the centuries. I think I'll be getting *Braveheart* out on video when I get home. Sky TV tracked us down at the Castle in order to bring a bit of Scottish flavour to their World Cup programme. After interviewing us, they decked out Harry in full Scottish regalia, including a kilt, for a televised skit where GA knighted Harry. ('Arise Sir Harry.' I thought I'd only ever see that in Christchurch.) Linda said she thought her hubby looked quite spunky in a skirt. **The funny thing was that Harry actually came to the Castle today with no underwear on beneath his tracksuit bottoms. So when he slipped on the kilt, he was a true Scotsman.** You can imagine the liberties that Harty and I took at the end of the skit for the benefit of the camera. We'll be watching closely tomorrow night when it screens to see how tight British censorship rules are.

Wednesday, June 2

ONE THING WORSE THAN a 5am wake-up call is sleeping through the call, waking at 5.30am and having 10 minutes to shower, pack, put the No 1s on, and make the bus. A bad start to the morning, and it only got worse. We were on an Edinburgh-to-Heathrow shuttle, which for starters left us sitting on the tarmac for 30 minutes before take-off. When we finally hit the air, the captain informed us that the weather was dicey in London and we'd have to spend an extra half an hour in a holding pattern before we could land. **It was a bit of a bumpy trip, not helped by one of the boys breaking wind regularly in his sleep.** Upon landing, the ground staff hadn't arranged enough buses to cart us across to Terminal One, so there was another delay. To top it all off, after we'd cleared our luggage we were stuck in a queue that didn't move for 15 minutes – there had been a fire alarm out in the terminal and they wouldn't let us out. We finally made it to our bus and it was straight off to Buckingham Palace to meet Liz.

Today was the only time throughout the tournament that a formal occasion involving all the teams had been organised. The timing was bad. Were in the middle of competition, and I knew I didn't really feel like talking to many of the opposing players. Not when I'd be trying to kick their butts over the next week or so. The 12 team buses all parked in the main courtyard of Buckingham Palace, and we were shown inside. The Palace is magnificent, the architecture, the furnishings, the portraits. **We had a few quiet royal orange juices, yarning among ourselves, and then right on 11.30am headed through into another room. And there they were, waiting for us, Queen Elizabeth II and the Duke of Edinburgh.** We shook hands with them both, saying the right words as we had been briefed ('Your Majesty' and 'Your Royal Highness'), and were moved into another room. No dramas, other than Fran being introduced as Carl Bulfin. He wasn't happy. Apparently Murray Goodwin from Zimbabwe missed being introduced with his own team and tagged onto the end of the West Indies team. When introduced to The Duke following the big fellows from the Caribbean, the Duke said, 'Well, you're certainly not from Jamaica,' to which Goodwin replied, 'I might not look like one, sir, but I'm certainly hung like one'.

I miss my mate Heath Davis when on tour. One thing for sure: Davo would always give you a laugh with his habits and humour. In fact, it was great to see Davo for a few beers after the Scotland game. He's playing league cricket in Northern Ireland, and flew over to watch the game and catch up with the boys. **Typical Davo, though. I had left four tickets out for him and his mates (the tickets are in short supply, as I've said) and he turned up only 10 minutes before the end of the game and with only two mates. He saw three overs and wasted a ticket. None of the guys were surprised.**

Back to Buckingham Palace, though, and I think we have an able substitute for Davo in Carl Bulfin. When the finger food was being passed around, Bully pigged out and found his hands had become pretty greasy. Instead of hunting down some serviettes, he reached for the nearest material, which happened to be one of the long, heavy velvet curtains.

All in all, I found it a damned boring experience. There were no speeches as we had expected, no photos of the teams, which was disappointing and, really, after taking in the grand surroundings, it was just standing around and chatting with team-mates. The Sri Lankans did try to liven up the occasion. **A couple of them tried sitting on an old antique table and promptly broke a leg off it, hitting the floor with a huge smash.** Two waiters quickly carried the debris away, and two very embarrassed Sri Lankans slunk away to the furthest corner. When you think about it, we were up at sparrow's fart this morning to travel from Scotland to London to essentially stand and talk to each other for two hours. With a five-hour bus trip back to Leeds tomorrow morning, it makes you wonder a bit.

Thursday, June 3

ON ARRIVAL IN LEEDS, the dirt trackers from the Scotland game had a compulsory practice. It had been raining, so we were restricted to an indoor bat and bowl, which is far from ideal when the game of cricket is played on grass. It's really just a matter of keeping the bat and ball in the hand to ensure that the sharpness doesn't drop away and that the skills are honed where necessary. The rest of the squad had a weights session in the gym, and that was it – one of those days that you look back on and think, 'There goes a day from my life.'

Friday, June 4

ON TOUR IT'S IMPORTANT to chill out on your own every now and then. The majority of this squad will be together for close on four months, which is a hell of a long time to be living in the same company up to 15 hours a day, seven days a week. So grabbing your own space is crucial. **One of the big benefits of the World Cup is that we all get a single room.** That's the chance to relax back with your own personal routines. There's no need to be concerned about the presence of a room-mate, you can play your music as loud as you want, the light and TV can go off at night when you wish, and your hygiene habits are your own. Not that having a 'roomy' has stopped a few filthy souls in the past. After nine years of having my kids waking me nice and early on a daily basis, I now find it hard to sleep in, as opposed to some of the younger guys who, I'm sure, are nocturnal animals. Normally I'm down at breakfast by 8am and enjoy a quiet breakfast reading the morning paper. **As Karen would testify, I'm not big on chatting over breakfast. She'll confirm that I'm not a 'morning person'. This morning I tried to steer clear of everyone.** I cleared my e-mails, wrote a couple of faxes, went to get a film developed, tidied up my playing gear and quietly started to get my head around the importance of the next game.

Owing to the unsettled weather, our practices have become a bit disjointed, and we again got stuck indoors at the Yorkshire Indoor School. The guys hate it, but you just bite your tongue and get stuck in. As a bowler, I find my legs and lower back take a battering on the hard surface, particularly after bowling on grass for so long. So it's human nature to take the foot off the pedal a bit, bowl within yourself, and look forward to your last delivery. Near the end, the word came that the weather had cleared and the groundsman had put up the nets. So we raced over to Headingley, threw the bowling boots on and got a few overs in on the grass. Invaluable, particularly for me as I hadn't bowled for over a week. Stumper then took the opportunity to put us through one of his fielding drills, and all I can say is, 'Thank God the rain came again.' **We were woeful. We misfielded everything, dropped catches, and the throwing was sloppy. The boys know Stumper and his body language well now and he was spewing.** We raced back onto the bus when the rain pelted down, and Stumper sat in his normal position at the front not saying a word. Already we weren't looking forward to tomorrow's practice.

THEN THERE WERE SIX

The local rugby league team, the Leeds Rhinos, had a home game that night and we were given complimentary tickets. Ian Robson, the ex-Warriors CEO, is in charge there and helped us out. Dan and Macca got into the spirit of the occasion, getting involved in the Leeds chants and enjoying themselves. Leeds were 30 points too strong for the Gateshead Thunder and the 10,000-strong crowd went home happy. **The Zimbabwe team was also there, and was quite interested in the game as many of them had never seen a league match before.**

The Aussies are worrying me a bit. They seem to be peaking nicely and today they dealt to India easily. Their key players are starting to front and they've settled on a balanced combination. McGrath is now firing with the ball, which is a danger for the opposition top-orders. They're not talked about over here as much as South Africa and Pakistan, the teams most people are mooting as the finalists, and I'll bet the Aussies just love that.

Saturday, June 5

WE TOPPED OFF OUR preparation with a morning practice. We were all waiting for Stumper's fielding drills and, sure enough, we weren't going near the nets until the fielding was right. We were all ready, though, and put on a show for the coach, with guys like Harry, Hornet, Macca, and GA leading the way. There was plenty of encouragement and communication, and lots of diving. All the coach could say at the end was, **'Why do we make things so bloody difficult for ourselves?' The guys hit the nets with a smirk.**

I used to really rate myself as a fieldsman, but now it's a real challenge to ensure that my skills don't let me down at this level. With the body getting older, I've found I need to do extra work to keep the sharpness and, in particular, the ability to get down to the ball quickly. I find the critical time is when I've finished a spell, cooled down and stiffened a little, and then need to produce something at speed. Flexibility is a key to me. I've done

Three hours and thirty one minutes of sheer torture... the Rotorua Marathon, 1989 (never again!)

a lot of work in this area over the last two to three years, and pride myself that I'm always near the top when the flexibility tests are done. I make sure I stretch every day and Body Control Pilates has been just great for keeping the body supple and in reasonable balance. Of course, stretching is just one component of the fitness requirements of playing cricket at the top level, and over the last five years, fitness training has become very structured. I relish that, and one thing in my favour is that I've always enjoyed keeping myself fit. I ran the Rotorua Marathon back in '89, played Central League soccer in my late teens, and interclub squash a couple of years ago. In fact, Mark Plummer, our old NZ team physio, actually banned me from playing squash on tour after I popped a calf in Lahore the day after an extremely hard game against Harry (both very competitive boys who hate losing). I blamed the 7am shuttle runs we were doing on a wet ground; Plums blamed the squash. We still beg to differ. Bottom line – I missed the '96 World Cup quarter-final v Aussie. I've also spent many an hour working out at Bodyworks Gym in Wellington, lifting weights and cross-training, and after my stress fracture in my back, I used a personal trainer (Wayne Marsters, who also works with the Wellington cricket team), to assist me in my comeback. One thing's for sure: when you use a personal trainer, there's no shirking. The cheque's in the post, Wayne!

Still on fitness, the famous Beep Test is normally dominated by Adam Parore, one of the fittest cricketers on the world scene. He does get rivalled, of course, as there are always pretenders to the throne. But Adam's guts and determination to hold onto his crown usually see him through. **The pretenders usually come in the form of Shayne O'Connor and Geoff Allott, both guys with a big aerobic capacity (and big hearts to boot). The sprint award is usually Dion Nash's,** a real athlete in every sense of the word, and the sprint and turn test (the run three with pads on) generally results in the hyperactive Chris Harris emerging No 1. I'm traditionally a mid-pack finisher in the tests, but will add that the hamstring stretch award does go to yours truly.

We had a bizarre situation at the end of practice. DJ pulled me aside and asked me if everything was OK, if I was happy enough or if I had any problems. I looked at him strangely, not knowing what he was getting at. He said that he had just received a call on his mobile from a New Zealand Sunday paper, asking if it was true that Gavin Larsen was returning home immediately. I just laughed and told DJ everything was

100 per cent fine and I was here to claim a World Cup winner's medal. DJ said he knew that was the case, and he had told the paper, **'Piss off and stop causing trouble. I'm watching Gavin at fielding practice now. He's laughing and enjoying himself. In fact, he's running around like a 21-year-old!'** I love the guy!

For God's sake, where do these rumours come from? There's one thing for sure: playing sport in the public spotlight makes your skin about three inches thick. During the same call, DJ was also asked if we had had a major disciplinary incident within the team. I can only hazard a guess as to what DJ's response would have been to that one. We've had four fines on tour, for minor dress and time-keeping violations, and the all-round discipline from everyone has been superb. The distinct lack of controversy is obviously annoying certain media boys.

Never say die must be the South African motto. Again today they were backed right into a corner in their match against Pakistan, and again that man Lance Klusener did the business for them with the bat. The Pakis froze, and Zulu used his three-pound bat to great effect. It was a mighty game that ebbed and flowed, and it was the South Africans' slightly greater desire to win that came through at the end. We watched the end of this game after our Captain's Meeting, at which it was apparent to me that the guys were relaxed and ready for Zimbabwe. Tomorrow is another major test. Zim are on a roll, and we all feel that we're playing well, albeit minus the runs that are required at the top of the order. **If we lose tomorrow, we make things very difficult for ourselves.**

Sunday, June 6

NEW ZEALAND V ZIMBABWE AT LEEDS
Zimbabwe   175 all out
NZ   70-3   Match abandoned

PEOPLE SOMETIMES RAISE THEIR eyebrows when I try to stress how difficult cricket can be mentally, and why that

THEN THERE WERE SIX

makes it such a great game. Today was certainly one of those days when your mental powers are tested to the max. **It was basically a 12-hour day in the office, and we didn't arrive back at our hotel until 8.30pm.** Bad weather and cricket seem to go hand in hand at times. The day dawned fine enough, with the toss going the way of Zimbabwe, who decided to bat first. GA again struck early blows and when the first rain came after 15 overs, Zim were 45-3 and on the back foot. Out came the cards, the books, the newspapers and the chat. Basically anything in an attempt to relax back and take the mind off the cricket. It can just blow your mind if you don't switch off.

We handle these breaks a lot better than we used to, when we tended to stress out a little, particularly if the interruption was in the second innings and run-chase adjustments were being made. 'Control the Controllables' is a wee cliché that is used by the team now, one of my favourites because it's very pertinent to cricket with all its external factors. There's one thing you certainly can't control and that's the weather. So we just try to chill out, and wait for the official word from the umpires or our management on start times and run-chase adjustments.

However, there are certain things that do need to be thought through during the break. In this case, I know that when we restart I'm bowling immediately at the Kirkstall Lane end. Campbell and Goodwin are batting, so I've got a left/right combination to combat and my adjustment of line becomes crucial. I'm not too sure about the nature of the wicket, as often things change a little with my medium-pacers as compared to the quicker deliveries of GA, Nashy, and Cairnsy. So I'll be trying to ascertain my ideal length as quickly as possible. It's also been raining, so damp run-ups will be a factor, as will a wet ball for a time. On top of that, the body cools down with an extended break so **I will need to go through the stretching routine again, along with a quick jog outside and a few deliveries to get the blood pumping again.**

Two hours later we're back to work, managing another 20 overs before the rain returns. More time in the changing room,

The gods are not smiling... Cairnsy in reflective mood at Headingley as the rain falls.

this time centred around Twosey picking the Cantabs' minds as to why they have been so successful over the last decade. There is much I admire about Twosey's game, not the least of which is his analytical mind. He is always challenging himself, looking to better his game, and is never afraid to ask questions. As captain of Wellington, he is extremely thorough in his preparation and is a 'players' captain', a leader who communicates well and gets on with everyone. The Cantabs take the piss a bit, particularly about Wellington's inability to land trophies with all our finals appearances. They ask regularly if the rope burns on our throats are healing OK? **We take it on the chin and I always sense in Twosey an unspoken ambition to beat the Cantabs in a final on their own Jade Stadium.**

We finally finished off the Zimbabweans for 175. They really struggled throughout owing to our tight bowling and sound fielding. GA, with his three wickets, has now equalled the World Cup record of 18 wickets in one tournament – just one more big man! He's been nothing short of brilliant throughout. We raced through to 58 off eight overs, then in our own inimitable style lost three quick wickets to put the pressure back on ourselves. Mind you, it was great to see Nath and Hornet spank it around early on and hit their way back into some sort of form. Flem and Twosey, after weighing up the match situation, the dim light and the state of the wicket, decided to accept the umpires' offer of bad light. At 70-3 it's even, but a good solid start tomorrow and we'll take this game away from Zimbabwe.

Monday, June 7

I DON'T WANT THIS to sound wrong, but after a day like this it makes you wonder what you have done to upset the cricket gods. A very, very depressing day, and an extremely bleak Headingley with rain drifting in for most of the day. The match was well-poised, with us needing a good first 10 overs from Flem and Twosey which would have assisted us getting through to our target of 176. The rain cleared on the odd occasion, briefly raising our hopes, but quickly returned to then drown them. **Again we spent the day attempting to amuse ourselves, but the underlying feeling all day was a negative one. We felt we were destined to take only one point away from the match.** The umpires put us out of our misery at 4.30, we shook the Zimbabwean hands (and I tell you it was hard to look them in the eye), and got out of that city as soon as possible. The ironic thing was that when we hit the M62 and left Leeds, the sun broke out. It almost made you cry. You don't want it to sound like sour grapes, but after 33 preliminary games with no washouts – why us in a game like the Zimbabwe match where the two points were so valuable? The other thing that chokes us is that the point the Zimbos get all but guarantees them a semifinal spot.

If we are to take positives out of the two days, then the first would have to be the way Nath and Hornet, playing some attacking shots, got themselves into some nick. The second would be the continuation of the pressure we've been exerting via our bowling and fielding. And the last positive, and the most important one, is that we still have our World Cup destiny in our own hands. That means almost definitely needing to win both our remaining Super Six games, and knowing the guys so well now, I know we'll approach this difficult task with confidence.

Over here, as I've stated often we're just not rated. Today in the *Daily Telegraph* newspaper there was an article written by a Turkey (and that's with a capital T) named Martin Johnson. It would have to be the most derogatory and patronising piece I've seen written on the New Zealand cricket team. It basically criticised our bowling line-up (a pretty damned effective one at this tournament, I would have said), which he called staid and without flair. **He asked how the public could possibly get excited watching Gavin Larsen bowling to Murray Goodwin (Zimbabwe), and said that a team having Larsen and Chris Harris bowling through the middle was bringing the game into disrepute.** He also dredged up for more use the ex-England coach David Lloyd's three-year-old quote about Nathan Astle's bowling: 'If Astle is an international bowler, then my rear end is a fire-engine.' If that is meant to be humorous then... ha, ha. Call me old-fashioned, but isn't part of the one-day game not only taking wickets but also restricting the opponents' runs by tight bowling? I'm not one to push my own barrow, but if playing 120-odd ODIs with 100 or so wickets and a runs-per-over rate of 3.7 is bringing the game into disrepute then I'm sorry, I should have retired years ago. Maybe part of dear Martin's problem is that the very similar bowling of Mark Ealham, Ian Austin and Adam Hollioake is no longer on show and he no longer has the chance to gloat about his quite marvellous England team. I've got a feeling I'll still sleep OK tonight.

Tuesday, June 8/Wednesday June 9

BIRMINGHAM, AND THE SWALLOW Hotel. Marvellous hotel, great staff, huge rooms, and a silver service dining room.

The England team normally stays here, so you know it must be posh. Talking about England, their lack of success on the park certainly doesn't equate with their top players' rewards off it. Their flash cars, big county and England contracts, huge bat and clothing endorsement fees, and lucrative benefit seasons tend to give it all away. I hope that doesn't smell of jealousy or narrow-mindedness, but **I must say that hearing that the England squad was involved in a contract dispute over money just before the World Cup started didn't really surprise us.**

Glenn McGrath made a really interesting point the other day. He said that defeat didn't hurt the England players enough, and I reckon there's an element of truth in that observation. Another interesting point emerged when a couple of our guys were yarning with one of the England players after their early exit. The type of comments that were made by the English player, about some of his own players, included, 'So and so doesn't play the short ball well,' and, 'So and so picks and chooses his batting position.' We have a great little saying that we use: 'In the belly, not the back' – if you're going to criticise someone, do it positively and to their face. Don't ram the knife into their back. Knowing how strong our team dynamics are now, I would be really surprised if any of our guys criticised a fellow player behind his back.

The tournament organisers have finally seen the merit in the quick bowlers' speed gun. Previously, it had been deemed too expensive to implement, but a sponsor emerged out of the woodwork. It's all happened owing to one guy, the Pakistani speed king, Shoaib Akhtar. And believe me, with that guy I'm happy I do my batting down at No 10. He's caused a real ripple over here and it's great for the game. Genuinely quick, he even had the audacity to suggest he could send one down at 100 miles an hour. That got the sponsor on board pretty quick. He's sending down his deliveries at a consistent 90 miles an hour-plus, and maxing out at 95, which is pretty damned rapid. GA has registered a few 90-pluses, and BA is next in the late 80s. I struggle! My stock standard, or so Harry tells me (and he never lets the truth stand in the way of a good story) is around 75 miles an hour. Mind you, Cairnsy did say he saw my effort ball register 85. Or did his smile give him away?

This is Twosey's homecoming. He spent many a year up here in Birmingham playing for Warwickshire, before he made what I guess was a tricky decision to leave the security of a very well-paid county contract, and the chance of playing for England, to start a new life in New Zealand. Warwickshire's loss has certainly been our gain. **After our arrival at Edgbaston, he spent his first half hour chatting with all his old acquaintances and spinning a few yarns.**

We know now that we must definitely win one of our remaining Super Six matches, and maybe both, to advance to the semis. We must take the South Africans on and back ourselves. That's how we approached the one-dayers back in New Zealand and we had some good results against them. One backward step tomorrow and we'll get nailed.

Thursday, June 10

NEW ZEALAND V SOUTH AFRICA AT BIRMINGHAM
South Africa   287-5
New Zealand   213-8   Loss by 74 runs

TOTALLY OUTPLAYED ALL DAY. After the South Africans decided to bat, we started well enough with some great ring fielding from Harry and Hornet. But once Kirsten and Gibbs got established, it was all downhill. We became quiet and never implemented the 'in-their-face' attitude that we wanted to. Our bowling was passive and we offered them two lengths all day. With wickets in hand they had a great springboard and finished off the innings by whacking 93 from the last 10 overs.

I remember Andy Roberts, the great West Indian fast bowler, saying that bowling was a bit like going fishing: 'Sometimes you catch some, sometimes you don't.' The art is in consistently picking the spot where the fish are. Today the fish didn't bite for me. In fact, the waters felt distinctly empty. I was a little off in my rhythm and lost my length as a result. And these guys need no second invitation. **On top of that, Kirsten and Gibbs, besides picking me off regularly for ones and twos, also invented well.** Kirsten played a couple of lap shots for four, which no-one has done before, and Gibbs played a couple of sweep shots which are normally reserved for spin bowlers. I enjoy the challenge when batsmen attempt to innovate against me. It raises the risks for them and opens up wicket-taking opportunities. However today was definitely their day.

The familiar story unfolded with the bat. Our openers nicked out again, and Macca got himself in and was ready to

GA. He held our bowling together for the whole tournament.

launch when he got himself out in a soft fashion. As usual, the South Africans were extremely competitive with their bowling and fielding, and the pressure they exerted told on our batsmen. The required run rate rose too quickly, and we trod water for the whole innings.

There's nothing worse as a bowler than to be batting way down the order, and for three and a half hours having to share a changing room with batsmen who've failed or are in the middle of a bad trot. There's nothing you can say to them other than giving them a 'bad luck' tap on the shoulder. Some will say nothing for the whole innings once dismissed; others return to normal a little quicker and you'll get some limited chat out of them. Some will let off steam when they're back in the hutch and I'm glad to say that we don't have any bat-throwers in the team. I've no time for them at all. You've also got the remaining batsmen who are preparing for their innings, awaiting their opportunity and who are constantly analysing the match situation. Some have headphones on, listening to music, others read a book or scan the newspapers. The bowlers will be found having physio or a rub-down from Fran. But it's fair to say that hardly a ball will be missed by anyone. There's always a TV in the changing room.

One of Stumper's rules is that everyone sits in the players' viewing area together, which encourages the boys to keep positive as a group. I've always been against that, as I find it so hard to sit in one spot and watch without getting a bit wound up. I'd much rather sit in the viewing area for a while, then drift back to the changing room, have a drink, watch a couple of overs on TV, chat to one or two of the guys, then head back to the viewing area after a period of time. Today was a bit different as the viewing area at Edgbaston is quite small and is right next to the changing room. You could also watch the game directly from the changing room so Stumper had no dramas that the team was split between the two areas.

We knew this would be a toughie. You need to be right on your mettle against these guys to stand a chance and we just didn't compete. They grabbed us by the throat early on and

THEN THERE WERE SIX

didn't let go all day. They're a great team who back their ability day in day out and have a one-day record that's the envy of every other international team. A 75 per cent success over 18 months is outstanding. It's a split choice between them or Australia as to whom I'd like to beat at Lord's on June 20. **But to get anywhere near the hallowed turf we need to dramatically improve our performance. If we don't, I'm winging it home in three days.**

```
Friday, June 11
```

ONCE AGAIN, AND AS the New Zealand cricket team does so well and so often, we've backed ourselves into a corner. We are now in a do-or-die position for the second time in this tournament. It's quite simple: we must beat India to make the semi-finals. India are now officially out of the World Cup, with Pakistan's huge win over Zimbabwe condemning them to a flight home on Sunday. That's another class team gone and there'll be hundreds of millions of Indian supporters around the world bitterly disappointed that their team have been eliminated.

I love playing the Indians. Their team is full of talented batsmen who bat with flair and it's always a great challenge bowling to them. The other thing I admire is their obvious enjoyment of the game. They're generally a friendly bunch and a smile is never far from their faces, yet, as you would expect, they are ultra-competitive on the park. That's the way cricket should be played. Touring India is also one of the great cricket experiences. **The people, the contrasting wealth and poverty, the landscape, the culture, the grounds and the fanatical crowds blend together to make such a tour unforgettable.** If there is one country that I'd like to spend more time in, it would be India.

At our debrief before departing for Nottingham, Flem showed to me how much he's grown into the captaincy with a really stirring talk to the team. It was an emotional address, aimed both at the team and certain individuals. I knew it had hit the right spot when the boys left the room. He said that we'd come too far in the last 18 months to throw it all down the gurgler, and that too few of the team had stood up and been counted throughout this World Cup. He highlighted GA and Twosey as the two guys to date who had shown the desire to make the difference, and urged us all to be one of the players to make the difference tomorrow. It was a spot-on demand from the captain that didn't fall on deaf ears.

Rugby commentator Grant Nisbett summed up our top order woes nicely. We were sitting back watching the All Blacks v NZ A match on Sky TV, with the ABs leading 12-3. 'That looks a bit like a New Zealand cricket scoreboard!' Nisbo commented. **Ian Smith jumped to our defence, saying that we were still in with a good chance tomorrow, and Nisbo was quick to agree.**

Saturday, June 12

NEW ZEALAND V INDIA AT NOTTINGHAM
India   251-7
New Zealand   252-5   Win by 5 wickets

I REALISE MY HAIR is slowly changing colour around the temples, and I can thank Ma and Pa, and their genes for that. However, matches like today make me understand why I've gone grey a bit prematurely. It was a brilliant result, a real nailbiter that took truckloads of hard yakka and commitment. The track was a good one at Trent Bridge, and 251 was probably a fair reflection on how the Indian innings went. Cairnsy and GA bowled well at the death, which has been a problem area for us, and saved about 20 runs with their tight bowling.

With India now out of the World Cup I suppose you could have forgiven many of the Indian supporters for staying at home today. Not these supporters, though. The ground was packed, the majority were Indians, and they were in party mode. I fielded in front of the noisiest section at one stage and couldn't hear myself think. There were drums and whistles and

THEN THERE WERE SIX

Trent Bridge, one of the great English cricket grounds, and the scene of our Super Six triumph over India.

bells – anything that could make a noise. It was great and made for a top atmosphere. Some of the English in the crowd didn't agree, though, probably those Nottinghamshire CCC members wearing cravats and drinking G-and-Ts. **There was an announcement at one stage by a pompous fishhead (the name cricketers affectionately call the administrators) over the PA system** that went something like this: 'We have received complaints from members that spectators in the lower part of the stand have been making excessive noise. This spoils the enjoyment of the game for other people watching. Could those spectators in that part of the ground please make less noise.' Well, excuse me, isn't this meant to be The Carnival of Cricket? You can imagine the response from the crowd. The volume doubled instantly.

When we batted, we got what we'd been waiting for for so long, RUNS FROM THE TOP ORDER! Not truckloads, but enough today. Nath and Hornet put on 45, with Hornet going on to a really valuable 74. Welcome back Old Gun! At 90-3, it

We're through! Me, GA, Nashy and Harry after the win over India.

was a touch dicey, but then entered our old (he's 31 now) middle-order pro, Roger Twose. And once again he added the cement to our innings. The next nervous period was when the rain came. It drove us off the park for close on an hour, an hour of wondering whether we'd be finishing late tonight or coming back tomorrow. But the skies cleared and we were left needing 58 off 10 overs at the restart. Cairnsy got out quickly, which brought Adam out to play one of the great cameo innings. He smashed 26 off 14 balls seeing us to victory in superb style. **The changing room was just bedlam. Another really special moment that will stay with me forever.**

We'd achieved what we knew all along we could – a date in the semi-finals. And that's not our lot. There are 200 overs left in this World Cup for us, not a lot of deliveries. I've played enough one-day cricket to realise that anything can happen, and that we were on the verge of something we'd cherish forever.

Semi-Belief

Sunday, June 13

I JUMPED OUT OF bed, grabbed the paper and turned to the sports section. Yep, we were still in the semis! A great feeling to think we are deservedly one of only four teams left in the '99 World Cup. We've been incredibly inconsistent with our performances, but when the real crunch times came we've shown great nerve and guts. To think that we have come nowhere close to our full potential is also exciting.

Chris Doig has arrived to watch the semis and final, and he sat out on our players' balcony yesterday with DJ, not missing a ball. I sat next to him at one stage and soon realised why none of the other players were sitting by him. He rode every ball that was bowled and his emotions would often get the better of him. **Watching the game as a player is nerve-wracking enough without having your CEO gasping at every second delivery! I lasted about an over before I moved back inside.**

Before Adam's innings yesterday, the boys had been pretty dark on him because of a real drop off in his wicketkeeping intensity. We didn't know if he was injured, or affected by some news from home, but he just hadn't been leading our fielding effort for the past two or three games. As I've said before, it's imperative to have your keeper buzzing, scrambling, talking and tidying up well at all times. Hopefully yesterday's great little innings will lead to him upping the ante with the gloves again, as he's a great keeper when he's firing. There's nothing better than Adam standing up to the stumps while I'm bowling and exerting his own sort of pressure via his excellent glovework and the chat he's famous for.

It does raise a point, though, about the type of off-the-park pressures that are placed on cricketers, and I guess all top sportsmen, particularly with all the overseas touring that takes place now. Pressures such as the media, your form, and the public expectations you learn to handle. **The type of pressures harder to handle are the personal ones. Marriages and relationships are certainly continually under pressure.** How couldn't they be when you're only a full-time partner for six months maximum every year? I'm incredibly lucky to have a wife as strong and supportive as Karen. There's no easy answer, but one could say with some justification that first-class and international cricket is a game for the young and single man. That is contradictory to my belief that a cricketer's best years are his late 20s/early 30s. I do feel our administration must start showing greater empathy in terms of our wives, partners and families. A box of goodies left on your doorstep by a courier at the end of the season with a 'thanks for your support' message is fine and it's a positive gesture. But maybe it's not quite enough.

As an example, a few days before going into camp at Lincoln to prepare for this tour, a letter arrived from NZC relating to the Shell Awards prizegiving evening during the camp. NZC was sorry, but wives and partners were not being invited. However, the Christchurch-based members' partners were free to attend if they wished. **If we wanted to bring our other halves, then we had to fly them down ourselves, and also purchase a ticket from NZC for the evening. Given that many of the guys were embarking on a four-month tour in a week, it was pretty insensitive.** Karen read the letter and promptly biffed it in the rubbish bin. A couple of the Christchurch players' partners were really embarrassed by the whole situation.

Things are hard enough without extra pressures being

SEMI-BELIEF

exerted by our administration. Chris Doig and the NZC administration have made excellent progress over the last three years. But this particular area needs some urgent attention. I'm seeing relationships becoming ever more stressed as our cricket commitments increase. The players don't expect the earth, but maybe something like a contribution towards airfares once a year so we can take our wives away on holiday somewhere where we don't have to be in cricket mode... that type of gesture would go down really well with the guys.

It can be bloody hard being stuck on the other side of the world while life is unfolding back in New Zealand. Just before our South African game, I found out that two friends back home – yes, two – have recently been diagnosed with cancer. Karen and I were pretty cut up when we spoke on the phone and my instant thoughts were that I'd rather be at home supporting my mates. All this on the evening before a crucial World Cup match. Naturally you have to be as professional as you can be and get on with the job in hand, but I'd be lying if I said I had a good sleep that night. You're only human and news like that is always going to affect you in some way. A little adjunct to all this was, due to my dismissal of Lance Klusener in the South African game, **I won $NZ3000 which was put up by** *The Sun* **newspaper as a bounty on Zulu's scalp.** It was to be donated to charity, and there was an obvious recipient given last week's news – New Zealand cancer research.

Other tragic news that I caught up on a few days ago centred around Winston Davis, who played for Wellington in 1990. His wife Trish gave me a call to tell me the terrible news that Winny is now a quadriplegic after a terrible accident while cutting trees for his local church in St Vincent. It happened about a year ago, and after three months in intensive care in the States and raking up a huge medical bill, it was confirmed that Winny would be in a wheelchair for the rest of his life. Trish and Winny battled British bureaucracy and finally the authorities relented and Winny will spend the rest of his time in England with 24-hour nursing. It seemed incomprehensible to me and all I could think of was Winny running in and bowling fast for Wellington a few years back. Trish mentioned that Winny wants to meet up with me and I'm going to do everything I can to do so before I head home.

It's hearing stories like these that just make you sit back a bit, have a little think about life, and put everything into context. It makes you think about the value of life, and the worth of living each day as if it's your last. Here I am in England, playing the sport I love, getting paid for it, and striving for success on the greatest cricket stage. I'm lucky, incredibly lucky. It also tells me that the best way to help my mates while here in England is to do everything I can in my cricket today and tomorrow to the best of my ability.

My life is revolving around attempting to win the World Cup, and not many cricketers in New Zealand get that opportunity. My news today confirms to me that I won't let it stress me out. If there's one thing I've learnt in cricket, it's that there's more to life than cricket. It's just not worth all the mental torture to think that cricket is the be-all and end-all. Being married and having three wonderful children running around also keeps me incredibly grounded, and there's simply nothing better than spending time with my family. They're all fit and healthy, and we're lucky.

A fantastic game of cricket has just finished. Aussie have just pipped South Africa with two balls remaining to clinch the last semi-final spot. In one of the best run-chases I've seen, they knocked off 271, via a superb innings from Steve Waugh, who smashed 120 not out. **I don't mind admitting that 'Tugga' Waugh is a real inspiration to me, and I'd guess to many other cricketers. His gutsy, hard-nosed, never-say-die approach to his cricket never ceases to amaze me.** All our boys were watching with avid interest, as the result determined our semi-final opponents. It means we play Pakistan at Old Trafford on Wednesday, and the Aussies have to do it over again against South Africa. Zimbabwe are eliminated, which I feel will please most people apart from Zimbabweans.

SEMI-BELIEF

Monday, June 14

A BRILLIANT TWO-HOUR BUS trip took us to our semi-final destination, Manchester. Why brilliant? Because Harty and myself made serious inroads into our euchre debt with Nath and the skipper. **The 80 pounds owing had been whittled down to 20 by the time we pulled into the Crown Plaza Hotel, and my partner and I left the bus high-fiving.** The TV crews there to greet us probably couldn't understand why our opposition were looking so downcast.

Today Twosey turned student. He sat a varsity exam for one of his finance papers, and it was overseen by DJ. Three hours of graft and, knowing the big fellow, he would have been

Twosey in champagne form... again!

thoroughly prepared. Adam is also doing a couple of law exams while on tour. It's great to see some of the guys preparing themselves for life after cricket. On that note, Cairnsy recently invested in a fudge (that's food, not hair-product) business in New Zealand, and here's some free marketing for BA: it's fantastic. A bonus for the boys really, as his product is regularly passed around the back of the bus.

Last night I was easing back in my room when Stumper rang and asked me to pop down to reception for a quick chat. I knew that management had just had a meeting and could guess what was coming. Harty and Bully were already with the coach when I arrived downstairs, so I knew I was correct. **Stumper told the three of us that we would not be staying on for the test match component of the tour, and as is his fashion, it was short and to the point.** I'd been told by Ross Dykes, the convener of selectors, before we left for England that all things being equal I'd be heading home immediately following the World Cup. I had no problem with that. I realise my test playing days, albeit the brief ones I had, are well over and my career will wind down wearing the one-day gear. I have established a bit of a niche in this team and I'm extremely comfortable with my role, which is what my skills have dictated over the years.

What I do look forward to seeing is the next batch of international bowlers come through and watching them develop at the top level. Guys like Shayne O'Connor, Carl Bulfin, Chris Drum and Andrew Penn are putting pressure on the test incumbents, and at the level below them there are another four or five bowlers making moves. **Exciting times, but is there a Shoaib Akhtar somewhere around the corner?**

At one-day level, I'll have a personal interest in seeing which way the middle-of-the-innings bowling tactics go when I lose my spot or my body tells me it's time to pack it in. There are different scenarios. Will we go with a more attacking option such as one of the quicker bowlers and get Nath bowling more? Will Dan be used more? Or will we perhaps go with a tighter slow option like Harty, who has an excellent RPO? The player I'd like to see establish a spot is Alex Tait, who, while he is quicker than me, is a guy who is always there and there about, and nips the ball around. He could play an important containing role through the middle stages of an innings. It boils down to Taitey's desire. As the saying goes, it'll all come out in the wash.

The guys I feel for are Bully and Harty. They've been brilliant on tour. At all times they've continued to show a great work ethic, even when they haven't been able to grab a regular spot in the playing XI. I know they are both gutted about missing out, a natural reaction when you have set your sights on remaining in the squad. The replacements are all logical ones. Matthew Bell to open the innings, Shayne O'Connor to open the bowling, Martin Croy to provide crucial support for Adam, and Brooke Walker to gain 'work experience' as Stumper put it, with his leg-spinners. Mixed emotions for both the dropped and the selected.

Tuesday, June 15

WE PRACTISED EARLY AT Old Trafford as the Pakistanis got in ahead of us and booked the nets for 11am. They've always been a bit disorganised with these types of thing in the past, so I hope that's not a bad sign. Practice was short and sharp and the boys worked hard for two hours. Immediately following every practice is the media's opportunity to grab the players and coach for comment. Flem and Stumper are, of course, always in demand, usually along with the form players. It was an amazing sight today as it seemed as if every TV, radio, and newspaper cricket journo was wanting to talk to someone. In fact, the requests for interviews have been so demanding that **DJ has placed a ban on interviews from lunchtime today, to assist the players to prepare properly. It confirmed the importance of our next game.**

After lunch, a group of us headed off to Old Trafford football stadium, the home of Manchester's favourite sons, in order to help kill off the afternoon. I was a bob each way really, almost feeling a traitor to the marvellous Liverpool FC, but I have to say that the two hours we had there were quite special. Upon entering the 'Theatre of Dreams', as they call the stadium, you couldn't help but acknowledge the size, the professionalism and the wealth of the club. **The tour guide threw plenty of facts at us, and at the end I was left with the impression that the saying 'the rich get richer' certainly holds true here.** The history of the club unfolded for us as we looked through their museum, and naturally photographs with the big three (the FA Cup, the League Champions Trophy, and the European Cup) were the order of the day. We viewed the pitch from one of the flash corporate boxes (there's a 10-year waiting list for these), had a look around one of the stands, checking out where both the supporters and the VIPs (and Posh Spice) sit, and then headed down to the players' areas. This is what I enjoyed: hearing about the players' routines on match day, seeing their dining room and after-match hospitality area, and their changing room. I sat where David Beckham changes, and couldn't help wondering if he'd be willing to swap jobs.

At the end of the tour we were strategically left just outside the Manchester United souvenir shop. They sold £30 million worth of merchandise last year, which is a bit hard to comprehend for a little old Kiwi who's involved in the sportswear game back in Wellington. **We popped in and had a look, the only buyer being Harry, who bought some Man U undies and wine gums. Thought you'd go for briefs, not y-fronts, though, H!**

Hundreds and hundreds of faxes have been flooding in, offering good luck messages for tomorrow. As usual they come from everywhere and everyone, and the feeling that I'm left with after looking through them is that we have our country right behind us. The overwhelming theme from back home is to enjoy the occasion, that we've already exceeded supporters' expectations, and that we have nothing whatsoever to lose. Again, it's a great reality check for the guys, and reading some of the faxes is quite emotional and inspiring.

SEMI-BELIEF

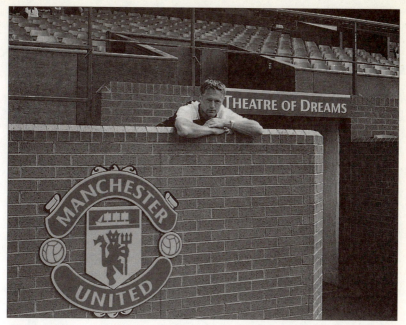

Old Trafford... could it, indeed, be our Theatre of Dreams?

Our team meeting was short. Flem pointed out that the team that absorbed and countered the pressure of the day best would emerge victorious. **The boys have all appeared relaxed and confident over the past couple of days, externally anyway. It's been noticeable that the chat and humour haven't diminished and the guys have been enjoying each others' company and haven't gone reclusive in any way. All good positives.** The key, as Flem rightly noted, is how we all manage these anxieties and to ensure that our arousal levels are held at a level that enables us to play at our best. It's one thing to be fired up for a match, but quite another when the adrenalin rush inhibits your performance. Bert calls it the 'Cooked Noodle' state. Flem finished off by stressing the need to treat tomorrow like any other match, to prepare in exactly the same way, and to make sure our personal routines remain the same. And, most importantly, to smile, enjoy the match and the occasion.

I have no doubt that the guys are mentally ready for the

game. As a unit, we've now played enough international cricket, and have enough experience built up to ensure that we don't stress out when the big occasion arrives. **The nagging doubt I have surrounds the inconsistent form of a few individuals.** I'm positive that we can win tomorrow, but only if we pull together something close to a perfect game.

Wednesday, June 16

NEW ZEALAND V PAKISTAN AT MANCHESTER
New Zealand   241-7
Pakistan   242-1   Loss by 9 wickets

IF WE WERE ASKED last night if we'd settle for scoring 241 batting first against Pakistan, the answer would have been simple. YES PLEASE! It's hard then to find the words to describe how I feel having turned around and lost by nine wickets. Hurt, ashamed, shattered, demoralised, embarrassed, gutted. I don't know – a mixture of the above, I suppose. It's left a real sick feeling in my gut. This was my last World Cup match, my final opportunity to achieve something that would make my cricket life unforgettable. I'll live this day forever.

We played half a good game. After scrambling and scrapping our way to 241, which was pretty much how we achieved our total, we let the Paki batsmen grab the initiative early on and never wrested it back. Our bowling was tame, we didn't grab the vital early wickets, and to be fair, Anwar and Wasti played superbly. They didn't put a foot wrong and really showed how a top order should operate on a flat wicket. We were positive at the lunch break; we knew we had a great opportunity and the mood was excellent. But it just didn't happen in the field.

Fielding down at third man early in their innings, I heard a Pakistani supporter yell out to me, 'Larsen, today will be just like '92.' What can I say now? He was right. The feeling at the end was similar, maybe not as emotional as '92 when we were playing in front of our home crowd, but still that distraught feeling.

SEMI-BELIEF

Thank goodness my old mate Rod 'Bunker' Latham wasn't here. I couldn't handle his tears again!

Another thing that is hard to describe is the level of Pakistani support at Old Trafford today. I'd guess that two-thirds of the ground was a seething mass of Pakistani green and white. It was like a home game in Lahore for them. How do they manage to secure that many tickets for the day? The noise while we were fielding was indescribable. They were generally quiet by their standard while we batted. They appeared nervous as the teams jockeyed for position. As we finished our innings they were as quiet as I've ever heard Pakistani support. They knew damned well that it was 'game on'. However, the party began when Anwar and Wasti arrived at their hundred partnership. The fireworks were released, which halted play for a few minutes, and the noise never diminished from there on. It was sign language only out in the middle.

The Pakistani supporter is passionate and emotional. While we were batting, one of their supporters walked past our viewing window and gave us the fingers. With the boys on a knife edge, something was always going to happen. Nashy

A sea of Pakistani support after our semi-final exit.

picked up a cup of water, biffed it through the window hitting the intended target (plus a number of other supporters, I must add! **Nashy should never have thrown it, but all in all it was a bloody good shot. The supporter tossed his toys out of the cot and grizzled to the nearest cops.** So we ended up having the boys in blue in our changing room, and the sergeant asked to see the captain. Doully couldn't contain himself and said, 'No problems. Just pop down through that gate. He's having a wee bat out in the middle at the moment.' The cop wasn't too happy. Rather ironically it was Nashy (our VC), who went with them to calm the situation down.

Towards the end of their innings it became quite apparent that there was going to be a crowd invasion, and to say I was bagging myself down at fine leg is an understatement. They were pushing forward over the advertising hoardings and with six runs to win, on they came. For 10 minutes chaos reigned as the security guys attempted to clear the ground to let the game finish. During the break, Hornet and I were sitting on the ground planning our exit strategy for when the final runs were scored. While we were outwardly laughing about it, deep down it's still a most intimidating situation and one that the players shouldn't have to be part of. **You can certainly understand why in India and Pakistan the supporters are totally caged in.**

I decided that swinging elbows were the best bet, and Hornet decided on the high stepping, run-over-anything-in-my-way style. He predicted that he would take out at least seven of them! The worst thing about it was that I was stuck down at fine leg, about 120 metres from safety. I guessed that I would meet the masses near the wicket, meaning another 70 metres of swinging elbows. I'm not the quickest cricketer around (Twosey and I are rated last equal over 100 metres by the team), so I called Flem over and registered my concern. I realise I'm nearing the end of my playing days, but I didn't really plan on going out at the hands of Pakistani supporters. The skipper was great. He just laughed. Thanks for the concern, pal! To his eternal credit, he did say that if the Pakis got one hit away from victory then to sneak in as far as I wanted. I took liberty with the word 'sneak', then as Anwar hit the winning runs I ran a sub-10 second hundred to make the safety of the changing room.

It was a very quiet and reflective changing room at the end. What can be said at a time like this? We hadn't grasped what was an exceptional opportunity. The tournament was over. All our one-day trousers, training shorts and shirts, and pads were tossed into the middle of the changing room. They wouldn't be needed again. Shirts were packed away to be signed up by the team as keepsakes or giveaways. And the food that got delivered into the changing room didn't have any taste whatsoever.

So the promoters will be happy. Little old New Zealand are out; Pakistan and all their support will now hit Lord's to take on one of the heavyweights, Aussie or South Africa.

Thursday, June 17

IT'S ALL SINKING IN now. We had a great chance and blew it. It's a hollow, empty feeling and I'm full of 'what ifs'. Last night I shared a few beers, first with Winston Davis's wife, Trish, and a couple of her mates, then with a good mate of mine from my league cricket days in Yorkshire, Chris Fisk. **Fisky was pretty depressed, too. I think he may have had some money riding on us.**

Cricket is the greatest sport in the world. If you witnessed today's Aussie v South Africa semi-final, then you'll know exactly why. It was a sensational game of one-day international cricket and probably, in terms of drama, the greatest I've seen. The stakes were huge – a spot in Sunday's final at Lord's. The drama that unfolded just couldn't be equalled. It was a day full of twists and turns, disappointments, brilliant performances and then a finish that no script-writer could possibly pull together.

Nine runs needed off the last over, South Africa nine down and Klusener smashes Fleming's first two balls for four. And I mean smashes. One to win and the World Cup star on strike. Only one possible result, surely. But never write off those Aussies. The next ball, with the whole field up, should have resulted in a run-out. Lehmann at mid-on misses the stumps from about a metre. Then another horrible mix-up between Klusener and Donald, and it's game over. The scores were tied and the Aussies make the final by virtual of a better position in the Super Six. **They were ecstatic, and I'm sure the South Africans were already stringing themselves up in the changing rooms.**

I was watching it in my room, and as the drama unfolded I could hear others in their rooms yelling out. At the completion, almost in unison we all opened our doors and gathered on the eighth floor hotel hallway to share the moment. The guys were all in various states of undress, and were all fired up and pumped after watching the finish. You may think that after our loss yesterday, we wouldn't give a toss about this game. I suppose it just shows you the type of grip this great game can have on you.

So the South Africans are out, cruelly and almost unfairly. The Aussies have stolen a spot in the final from under their noses with two extraordinary wins. I feel for them. They are polite and humble off the park, have a great leader in Hansie, and are excellent ambassadors for the game. They let their performances do the talking. This World Cup was to be the culmination of two years of great one-day cricket, and a goodbye gift to their departing coach, Bob Woolmer. But I also have firmly in my mind the thoughts of a number of their supporters I've knocked into over the tournament. Theirs was a super-confident feeling that they were destined to win this World Cup, that their record was second to none, and a hiccup or two was not going to stop them lifting the Cup. In Birmingham, after our thrashing at their hands, a patronising supporter said 'bad luck' to me with a smirk on his face. I remember thinking to myself at the time, 'Don't go counting your chickens yet, mate.' For cricket has this amazing way of kicking you when you least expect it.

Friday, June 18

WE GATHERED AS A squad late in the morning for an autograph signing session and a tournament debrief. The guys arrived with shirts, bats, stumps, and even, in Fran's case, his physio table, to be signed by the World Cup squad. It's a tradition to get your gear signed by the team, for keepsake purposes, or as giveaways for the likes of charity auctions. Signed memorabilia is in huge demand, and I'd say I'm asked on average once or twice a week if I have something I can donate to a charity. Many of the guys are collecting gear now for when their benefit seasons roll around with their respective associations. Bully had an old bat that he spent ages cleaning up, getting it ready for signing up by the four semi-finalists. Once it was nicely tidied up, he then ruined all his good work. **In big bold letters in black marker pen he wrote '1999 World Cup Semi-Finalists'. However, he spelt Finalists as Finilists. The boys loved it.**

Bert had called the debrief as he felt that at the end of a competition or tournament often that's just it. The team immediately disbands and thoughts turn automatically to what is around the corner – in this case the test tour of England, without any formal reflection. He got us all to give ourselves a mark out of 10 as to where we were at mentally and to list our team and individual highlights, as well as our major disappointment of the tournament. The marks ranged from a three through to a 10. The higher marks were from those who have put the semi-final disappointment behind them quickly and included some guys who obviously haven't played much and are jumping out of their skin to get the playing gear on.

I marked myself a three. I'm still struggling to come to terms with what we could have achieved, and, coupled with the fact that I leave the group tomorrow, I'm pretty negative on things. Bert

Poise, balance, style... a promotion up the order for Gav in 2003?

always facilitates these sessions well and the guys are upfront and honest with their thoughts. He also did a little exercise with us, getting us to concentrate on the differences between the negatives and the positives. He stressed we tended to fixate on the negatives. **The positives, of course, are the successes we've enjoyed over the last six weeks which we will cherish forever. He urged us to focus on the positives.**

Ray, our liaison guy, and Kevin, the baggage man, were then invited in and Twosey in his eloquent fashion thanked the two of them for all their sterling work throughout the cup campaign. Both these guys have become part of the extended family, and have been tireless and uncomplaining in their efforts to ensure everything ran smoothly. Ray heads back to Southampton, where he sits on the cricket committee at Hampshire CCC and in what I thought was a marvellous gesture by DJ, NZC are going to pay for Ray and his wife to

SEMI-BELIEF

spend the last week of the test tour with the team before they head home. The boys accepted Ray and Kev into the fold really comfortably, and Ray commented that he'd had an unforgettable six-week experience, something that hadn't been shared by a couple of the liaison guys with other teams. There's one thing about us Kiwis – we're a friendly bunch!

At the end of the debrief, DJ also said a few words, saying we must be proud of our achievements, and should enjoy the fact that we made the semi-finals. But, he said, the team now had to look ahead to the new challenge of the test tour. He finished by thanking Harty, Bully and me for our contributions. **Harty is taking up a pro's job for Wigan up in Lancashire, and Bully is staying on for a month or so with his girlfriend.**

The South African and Aussie teams rolled into the hotel this morning and the contrasting looks on their faces were quite dramatic. All four teams are staying at the hotel in Kensington, with everyone heading off to a formal Lord Mayor's function tonight with the Duke of Edinburgh attending. I knocked into Damien Fleming and Paul Reiffel in the lift. Surprise surprise, they were pretty upbeat following their win. I must say that they were also quite humble, saying it was the greatest game they'd played in and… wait for it, that they felt for the South Africans. As if they meant that!

Shane Warne was quoted in the paper this morning that given the way they've scrapped their way out of some tight spots in this tournament, they're destined to lift the cup skywards on Sunday. Knowing Warney, I'm not surprised at these words, but mate, I just hope you're not tempting fate. He was sensational yesterday and really stuck it up a few of the critics who've been on his case. **The South Africans were cruising it, and Warney was Tugga Waugh's last ace to play. And he fronted. It was inspiring and he single-handedly lifted his teammates and turned the game the Aussies' way.** To me, the big games on the big stage are when your star players need to stand up and be counted. To produce the goods. And boy he did.

I thought I'd do the right thing this afternoon and make

sure I spruced up OK in my No 1s for tonight's function. So I got the iron and ironing board brought to my room and hit my suit and white shirt with gusto. Karen will laugh when she reads this. **For starters my DIY skills have always been questioned around the home, although I always point to the valve-grind on my old mini as proof that Tim the Tool Man has nothing on yours truly.** There are two things around the house that you just won't find me doing. One is sticking my hands down the toilet and cleaning it; the other is that worst task on earth: ironing. Creased shirts and trousers are the norm on tour, so today was something special.

My ironing effort was all to no avail, though. We arrived downstairs at 6pm to find the lobby full of function attendees all looking splendid in their glad rags. However, a rumour was circulating that the night had been cancelled due to riots in the centre of London. We took a seat in reception, and sure enough, it was soon confirmed by one of the tournament organisers. Apparently today in England was affectionately known as National Demonstration Day and the anarchists of London had decided it was their opportunity to cause some carnage. They demonstrated about a number of things, Third World debt, capitalism, anything that gave them the chance to biff a few petrol bombs around and close down the centre of London. The police decided that it was too dangerous for the dinner to proceed, so that was that.

As we gathered downstairs Flem, Doully, and Twosey burst through the front entrance of the hotel, golf clubs in hand. They'd had an afternoon golfing, but had been caught in a traffic jam heading home. They were about 10 minutes away from a £30 fine each. We knew at this stage that the evening had been cancelled, but that didn't stop us from winking at each other, and letting them race upstairs to throw on their No 1s... and by the way, they weren't late.

The players from the four teams weren't crying that the function was off. It was the last thing we needed at this stage – to bring the two beaten semi-finalists and the finalists together at a social occasion. Not for me. The administrators and other invited guests were disappointed, and to be fair I'm sure it would have been a memorable occasion for them. **The tournament organisers opened up one of the function rooms at the hotel and put on an open bar, with the NZ boys needing no second invitation.**

I was off home at 7am the following morning, so I was going to enjoy my last night in London. Many of the guys and partners met up in a bar that's become one of our favourites over the years, the Cuba Club in Kensington. We had a good time and things became a bit of a blur from there on in. We left and ended up at a spot somewhere near our hotel – all I remember was dancing at one stage and looking up and seeing no familiar faces at all. The boys had deserted me. I had walked into a black tie function that was a charity event raising money for cerebral palsy and I'm guessing I looked a bit out of place with my jeans and untucked shirt, dancing among everyone in their evening-wear. Good fun, though.

Friday, Saturday 19

THREE HOURS' KIP, A raging hangover, and 36 hours of travelling in front of me. Not a good mix. Bert is also heading home for a three-week break before flying back for the test series, so I have a travelling buddy, which will be good. Very organised is Bert, and he was tucking into a full English breakfast when I got downstairs. I couldn't face food. **It was no surprise to me that DJ was down to say goodbye. He's got a real tough streak to him, but there's also a huge heart inside that chest of his, and he got a bit choked up when it came time to shake hands.** It made me realise how lucky we've been to have a guy with his qualities managing this team for the last three years. A few people won't agree with that, more than likely a few media guys who have rubbed DJ up the wrong way. He doesn't suffer fools at all, or people who have unrealistic expectations of the players, and it certainly doesn't pay to get on the wrong side of this man. He's going to be a huge loss when he leaves his post at the end of the England tour, and if NZC secures anyone remotely close to DJ's standard, then they'll have done well. I have full admiration for what he has achieved.

We hit Gatwick and, oh joy, found that we had to share Business Class with the South Africans. They were pretty good, though, still a bit downcast. A few of them looked how I felt – crook. Again we were fulfilling the sponsor's requirements by flying Emirates home. We have seven hours in transit in Dubai, and another seven in Singapore. A right pain in the butt.

While in the transit lounge in Dubai, a number of the staff and other passengers came up wanting to talk about the cricket. Bert and I were dressed in civvies, but they recognised my face. They were a mixture of personalities – Arabs, Indians, Iranians – all cricket fans who'd followed the World Cup with interest. **You really do begin to understand the global nature of our sport and in particular the huge influence TV has in bringing the game into living rooms all around the world. It's also a little mind-blowing for the little old medium-pacer from Onslow!**

Well, before I know it the realities of domesticity will be upon me again. My six weeks in the World Cup sun is over, the time on the cricket centre stage complete. It's back to dropping the kids at school, filling the car with petrol, taking Corey to rugby practice, shopping at Big Fresh, reading good-night stories to Vanessa, digging post-holes outside (yuk!), watching Nadia at her swimming lessons, and sharing a wine or two with Karen. And I can't wait.

Looking Back

IT'S SIMPLE. THE NEW Zealand cricket team made the semi-finals of the 1999 World Cup in England. We achieved something special. When presented with times of adversity we showed on a number of occasions the courage, commitment and skill to emerge on top. We dug deep when it really mattered and showed that we had the guts and the determination to succeed. Against Australia, Scotland, India, and for half a game against Pakistan in the semi, we showed New Zealand supporters what they wanted to see. And that was a team that fought and scrapped every inch of the way.

I feel extremely proud to have been part of this team. We have finished this World Cup more successful than higher-rated, and probably more talented teams, such as India, England, Sri Lanka and the West Indies. Yet I believe the best four one-day teams made the semi-finals. To me, Australia, South Africa and Pakistan are the three best teams in one-day cricket and very little separates them. They are truly great sides. Then come India and New Zealand, and then the rest. **But man for man, if we are deadly honest, we struggle a little when stacked up against the other test-playing nations, excluding Zimbabwe. It's spirit and commitment, plus heaps of hard work, that see us through.** Now we also have self-belief, the vital ingredient that I think has often been missing from New Zealand teams in the past.

We experienced good times and bad, but at all times we stayed true to our vision, and remained committed to our systems and philosophies. We had fun, which I hope is obvious from the diary, and we also worked extremely hard at our game. The work ethic was always excellent and training was never a drag.

Still I can't avoid a feeling of 'unfinished business' – a sense of unfulfilled promise. **When I look at the individuals within our team, how they performed and their statistical results, I am left with a feeling of under-achievement.** The squad's external message to the public right from the start was 'understate and overachieve'. We can safely tick off 'understate'. If I objectively mark everyone out of 10, I can bring myself to mark only four of the guys six or higher. And yet we made the semi-finals! If we'd come even close to maximising the talent in the team, we could have gone the whole way. And that leaves me feeling frustrated.

It was obvious to all and sundry that our big deficiency was in our top-order batting. There's no way any team will win a World Cup if it is consistently losing two or three early wickets. Both Nath and Macca struggled for the whole tournament and Hornet and Flem didn't churn out the runs that we all know they can. This put huge pressure on the middle order and luckily we had Twosey to rely on. He was superb throughout. The bigger issue was that we didn't have a specialist batting replacement in the squad, and the decision by the tour selectors to move Harty up to open against Scotland just exaggerated the problems with our out-of-form top-order. I found myself thinking that our squad had a late-summer, dry-wicket look about it. **You didn't have to be Einstein to work out that having two left-arm spinners sitting on the sideline (Dan and Harty didn't bowl a ball between them) was a waste of a spot.** Particularly when you factor in the obvious conditions we were going to face in England in May.

Our bowling was steady throughout, without setting the world on fire, excluding, of course, big GA. He was exceptional and was the cutting edge to our attack all

GA and me... two 'quicks' take a stroll around Arundel.

tournament. **As a bowling unit I thought things got a little 'tired' towards the end and inconsistency of line and length crept in. That certainly applied to me,** and although the stats were OK, I was disappointed with the way I tailed off in the last two games, when it mattered so much. If you analysed the big three teams, they each had a number of attacking, match-winning bowlers. Australia has McGrath, Warne and Fleming. South Africa has Donald, Pollock, Klusener and Kallis. Pakistan has Akhtar, Akram and Saqlain. We had GA, and when the time came to produce something exceptional in the semi-final, we couldn't.

We also talked a lot early on about being innovative in our tactical approach. It may appear to be hindsight, but maybe when it came to the semi it was time to be different, to try something new. The track looked dry and as if it had plenty of runs in it. Playing a spinner must have been a big option. Batting Raz, with his good technique, at three against Akram

Yes Lance, you're out! I've just dismissed South Africa's master blaster for the first time at the '99 World Cup.

and Akhtar must have also been an option, and that would have opened up the extra bowling spot. From a selectors' viewpoint, it was probably more that the dirties hadn't played for so long that made the risk too high to consider change.

So my World Cup experiences have come to a close. The big picture says I should be happy with the results: semi-final in '92, quarter-final in '96, semi final in '99. But no, I don't feel happy. Not in the slightest. I feel a degree of satisfaction with what we achieved, but real disappointment in terms of what should have been. Defending 262 at Eden Park in '92, Hogan pings his hammy, the Pakistani run rate reaches nine an over, and we blow it. Defending 287 in Madras in '96, I'm watching from the stand with a blown calf, and Mark Waugh and Co steal the game from us. And now the '99 story. People have asked me since I got home who I wanted to win the cup, Aussie or Pakistan? Easy answer. Neither. I wanted to be part of the parade down Queen Street.

Jobs For The Boys

ON EVERY TOUR THE manager allocates a number of tasks that are to be looked after by the players. When the manager reads out the duties, the players hold their breath as there are a few that are considered undesirable. The duties for this tour were allocated by DJ along the following lines:

Finance – Geoff Allott
GA's got a banking background so this one always sits easy with him. His main task was to dish out and register the daily allowance paid to the players. This money was to cover meals and laundry, so the boys were always keen for the laundry man to strike up good deals with the hotels. GA's other task was the splitting up of any prizemoney won, a task the boys love him for.

Laundry – Craig McMillan
Mmmmmm. A pain in the butt job, really, and normally given to one of the new boys. The idea, as I've said previously, was to strike the best possible deal with the hotels, to say nice things to the laundry ladies and to offer them signed shirts, etc in return for using their machines or getting a cheap deal. Didn't always work though, as we found on this tour. **Maybe it was Macca's way of making sure he never got given the job again, a bit like fielding close in under the helmet.**

Nurse's Aid – Matthew Hart

Our physio, Mark Harrison, carries about 10 bags around with him and obviously needs a hand or three when we're in transit. Harty drew the short straw on this one. Not a great job when you're forcing your way through crowded airport terminals.

Dress – Nathan Astle

The neatest, tidiest, best-groomed and snappiest dresser in the team had to get this job. **Attempted to stamp his authority, but there was a feeling in the team that poor old Nath was undermined by the old war-horse, DJ Graham.** I'm sorry DJ, but the brown checked shirt with the brown No 2 trousers you insisted on for

Nath – the neatest, tidiest, best groomed... mmm?

JOBS FOR THE BOYS

our travel from Edinburgh to London did not hang well on fit young sportsmen (that includes me, by the way). And Nath, you were far too soft with DJ. A prime source of fine money for the social committee, a couple of examples including Bully being caught in the gym wearing non-CCC branded socks, and (you'll like this one) Stumper going to meet the Queen in two-tone brown boat shoes when our No 1 shoes are black leather. Maybe it's an Australian thing. Their fashion sense has never been crash hot.

Flag and Scorebook – Carl Bulfin
The worst job in the team, and traditionally goes to one of the new fellows. Your memory is called into action before and after every match, as the flag and scorebook need to be taken to the ground, then picked up after the match. We've had some shockers in the past, with social committee funds always bolstered from this area. **On this tour, Bully had a blinder. Tony, our official scorer, who travels everywhere with us, took full control of the flag and scorebook. Very, very lucky Bully, because you would have been absolutely hopeless.**

Fines Master – Adam Parore
As I've previously mentioned, this appointment is an ironic one. One thing's for sure, Adam was a stickler for detail. You daren't be one minute late for the bus or that was £30 down the gurgler. **When he announced fines on the bus, he did it with real pride and gusto,** no doubt thinking back to all the times he's been pinged on tour. It was payback time.

Social Committee – Roger Twose, Gavin Larsen, Daniel Vettori
What a team. A mix of youth and experience, common sense, entrepreneurial flair, and Italian bravado. Our main task, when time allowed, was to organise team events in order to exhaust the accumulated funds of the social committee. With the advent of the Mini Teams on this tour, it's fair to say that the opportunity for full team events was

slightly limited, or that was our excuse anyway. The phrase, 'Do we actually have a social committee on this tour?' often rang out on the bus.

Before the tournament started, I organised a competition between the Mini Teams based on the World Cup Fantasy League in one of the newspapers. Each team drew up their tournament Dream Team, and then started accumulating points for their players' performances. Runs, wickets, catches, economy rates, etc. It was interesting to note that three of our four mini-teams put GA into their line-ups, an interesting reflection on how we perceived the big man and our expectations of what he might produce. The team that didn't pick him? I'll let you guess that one. **One hundred quid was up for grabs at the end of the tournament. I kept all the results, which gave the Parramatta Eels a huge opportunity.** Not surprisingly, we sprang out to an early lead, but were slowly hauled in by the Allott-led Stunned Mullets. The Spice Boys made progress up the ladder and, as expected, the Hart Throbs were mud. Rock bottom. In fact they were officially known as the Mud Throbs, and as I suggested could happen, in-fighting decimated this very poor team. Unfortunately the Mullets took the money.

Tickets – Simon Doull
Sensational performance all tour. **As you could imagine friends, ex-friends, and unknowns came out of the woodwork in an effort to snare tickets for the matches.** But Doully stayed strong, and juggled the varied requests with gusto. Twosey took the personal honours with a request for 10 tickets for Edgbaston, and good old Spike managed to come to the party. On a personal note, it was great to be able to help out my Wellington (and ex-Wellington) team-mates on a regular basis. Richard Petrie, Chris Nevin, Mark Jefferson, Glenn Jonas, Heath Davis and Stephen Mather all made a few of the matches and gave the boys really great, old-fashioned New Zealand support.

Timekeeper – Dion Nash

There's one moment that the boys love on tour. When anyone is late for a meeting or the bus or anything else, it means a £30 fine. And, of course, that helps the social committee funds. **So Nashy was a popular man, and as the clock ticked down towards meeting or departure time, and someone hadn't fronted, the boys would get quite excited.** Like a shark around blood! Nashy would produce the countdown (he has the official time on his watch) and upon the time passing the boys would yell, as an example only, 'Larsen... GONE!'

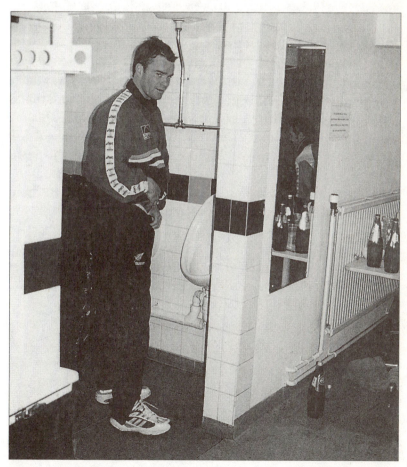

When you've gotta go, you've gotta go. Nashy at Headingley.

Transport – Chris Harris

Harry's official job on this tour was transport. Part of our liaison man's role was of course to organise all transport requirements for the team. So Harry was redundant and didn't he love it. Normally the transport guy would assist DJ where necessary in terms of checking in at airports, the collecting of passports, dishing out of boarding passes, liaising with the bus driver for any requirements over and above the standard team ones, and while on tour in New Zealand keeping track of the keys for the mini vans that the team uses. **So as you could imagine, Harry was a happy little camper and was idle all tour.**

Rooming list – Chris Cairns

Another idle man. **This World Cup saw everyone in the squad have a single room. Bonus! The boys were stoked that Cairnsy was made redundant.** Normally this guy would pull a list of room-mates together and fax it through to our next hotel. I've done this job a couple of times and it's a handy job in which to make a few perks. Often my phone would ring, and there'd be a whispered voice of another player on the other end. Questions along these lines would be asked . . . 'Would it be possible to room with so-and-so, I'm keen to talk to him about a few things?' or, 'We've got a test match coming up (7 or 8 days together) so could you wangle a quieter room-mate for me?' or even, 'Could you keep me clear of so-and-so, his snoring is just atrocious!' Well, every man has a price!

Meet The Cast

Stephen Fleming

It freaks me a little to think that Flem is still only 26. I remember his first tour, to England in '94, when we celebrated his 21st birthday. Even back then you'd have thought that Flem had been around the scene for years, and he's certainly taken to international cricket like a duck to water. He's probably the most natural timer of the cricket ball I've seen in New Zealand, and as most bowlers would testify, almost impossible to bowl to once he's in and away. **Of all the batsmen I've played with over the years only Martin Crowe would be more gifted.** Hogan was just the best in my eyes. Flem's also a great catcher – those huge slabs of meat on the ends of his arms (I think they're called hands) do tend to help.

Flem's probably disappointed with his batting returns at this World Cup. We saw only glimpses, although in the semi he was well on his way and into the 40s when Shoaib Akhtar propelled a missile into the base of his leg stump. One of the balls of the tournament. Flem's going to be around for years. A top man.

Enjoys: Reading novels, having a beer, golf, buying trousers.

Dion Nash

Our vice-captain. It's brilliant to have Nashy back in the fold, as his competitiveness brings so much to the team. There's nothing wrong with a bit of mongrel dog and D has it by the truckload. He stands eyeball-to-eyeball with the opposition and he has one quality I think is priceless: he hates losing. After the semi-final, D just sat in his corner, distraught, and didn't move for ages. His bowling was sound through most of the tournament. He proved a great foil to GA, who was taking wickets at the other end, particularly in the earlier games.

The fight in Nashy is evidenced by his comeback to international cricket after his bad back injury. It's a long road back. I know – I've been through the same grinder. No-one in our team would work harder on his batting. Batting down at nine, you could understand it if Nashy eased off the pedal a little. It's a trap I've certainly fallen into. But not D. He works as hard as any of the top-order boys, and often he'll be the last to leave the nets. **When the time is right, D will always be seen out with the boys, and he knows how to let his hair down. When he gets that spark in his eye and that smile starts, you know there's going to be action of some sort.**

Enjoys: Winning, confronting the opponent, massages, Pilates, nipple-pinching.

Nathan Astle
This just wasn't Nath's World Cup. The seaming wickets undid him early on and then, as the wickets dried out, he was just too deep into that horrible downward spiral we all experience at some stage. We all had the same thought – 'form is temporary, class is permanent' – and we were all waiting for the day when he would explode into action. Through the Super Six period he started whacking it really well in the nets, but it just didn't happen in the middle. Nothing really fazes Nath – that's one of his great attributes – and it was great that he kept his chin up and trained hard. **His lady arrived through the Super Six and his smile was huge then.** Nath's got a great one-day record for New Zealand, and I know this tournament will be only a small setback for him.

Nath's a perfectionist, one of the neatest and most organised cricketers around. Well-groomed. His gear is also exemplary, and to top it all off, he doesn't sweat. Saw him get a hundred in 35 degrees in India and there wasn't a bead on him. If that was me I'd have lost 5kg.

Enjoys: Table talk at euchre, looking smart, tidy gear.

Matthew Horne
The Old Gun. Nath's opening partner, who also suffered from, as he put it, 'having to deal with a few demons in the head' through the World Cup. Started with a 30 not out against Bangladesh, but then fell into the common 'nick the ball into the slips' top-order syndrome. His confidence went a bit (bloody easy in this game, believe me) and it wasn't until the Super Six that we saw the bubbly old Net return. His 74 against India, anchoring our innings, was a great knock. Would be uncommon to see Net walking around the hotel without a bat in his hand, and he arrived to our debrief in London wearing pads. **If you room next to Net and the walls are thin, then the tap, tap, tap of him taking guard in his mirror can drive you bananas.** A great team man, I find his sense of humour quite infectious.

Enjoys: Batting, music, hot pools, and batting.

Craig McMillan
This World Cup would probably represent Macca's first string of failures. He's had a superb start to his international career, and once he works his way through the short ball issue he's having, I'm sure he'll go on to be one of our best. The quality international quickies seem to have him sorted out a little at the moment, but knowing Mac, he'll work hard and get things moving forward again. As with Nath, he has all the ability in the world, and he has to channel that ability when the going gets tough, when the opposition are hammering him and not giving him anything to hit. **When he masters that, watch out world cricket. He's a Cantab, so he doesn't lack self-belief either.**

As we all know, Mac is a diabetic, which to all intents and

purposes is irrelevant to us the majority of the time. **However, there has been the odd time when his body has gone into shut-down mode while out with the boys. We've learnt that the sweat on his top lip is the giveaway.** So we have to race around and find something sweet for him to eat to top up his body sugars again. It happened towards the end of the tour and the boys said Mac was abusing punters on the street. They said it was hilarious, but Mac didn't remember a thing.

Enjoys: Sleeping, casinos.

Roger Twose

I've already used up my stack of superlatives on Twosey in the diary. He didn't put a foot wrong all tournament. I've got to know The Pimple pretty well through our time together at Wellington and I knew something special was just around the corner. He had set himself for this World Cup and once Twosey has a goal in mind he's a hard man to distract. He was driven, he was extremely disciplined with his preparation, and I think he had a statement or two to make to a few people. He was the consummate professional. If all cricketers took a leaf out of his book they'd be far better off for it.

Roger's girth is the subject of much ribbing in the team. He takes it well – I guess he has no option, really. The boys were tickled pink when they saw that Twosey had been selected by one of the bookies as part of a World Cup 'Who ate all the Pies?' spread bet. Gamblers had a chance to pick their 'big guy', and points were awarded if their choice ate or drank while on the park, if they left the park injured, if they needed a runner while batting, or if they were run out or dropped catches. The other 'big guys' were Shane Warne, Ian Austin, Inzamam-ul-Haq, and Arjuna (The Chef) Ranatunga. My choice would be with The Chef, the biggest showman to ever set foot on a cricket field. As for Twosey... well, he let his bat do the talking. Fantastic tournament.

Enjoys: The sharemarket, golf, massages, asking questions.

MEET THE CAST

Some of the cast during the making of the 1999 World Cup. From left: Hornet, Dan, Bully, Nath, Macca, Doully and BA in front.

Chris Cairns

The changes I've seen in Cairnsy since I first played alongside him have been quite dramatic. **There were times a few years ago that I'd have to say I didn't enjoy what I was seeing, and BA himself puts up his hand on this note. The new model has surfaced in the last couple of years.** Professional, committed, and really wanting to win games for New Zealand. This World Cup gave BA another opportunity to express himself as one of the prime all-rounders in world cricket. Unfortunately, he started the tournament a bit underdone with his bowling, the result of blowing a calf towards the end of our home season. As a consequence, we never quite saw the best of BA's bowling and he spent many an hour with Shotty getting things right technically. He played two great knocks for us, one against Aussie in combination with Twosey, then in the semi as we fought our way through to a competitive score. He showed great composure in these innings. BA's a real senior pro now and will be a crucial component of this team over the next couple of years.

Enjoys: Smashing sixes, socialising, fudge.

Adam Parore

Raz would undoubtedly be one of the most talented cricketers I've played with. It seems as though he's been around for donkey's years and has a mortgage on the keeping spot. And as he's a crucial batsman in our lineup, he's a genuine all-rounder. Raz plays his best cricket when he exudes that chin-up, confident body language. **However, we lost his keeping through the middle stages of the tournament and we only got the bubbly guy back after his brilliant knock against India.** Raz and myself are the two Slazenger-sponsored players in the team. This can be very handy as Raz always has a good relationship with the sponsors, including the knowledge of the right people to hit for the free gear!

Enjoys: Law, sleeping, fast cars, finance, socialising.

Chris Harris

Harry reckons he's got another two World Cups in him. Well,

MEET THE CAST

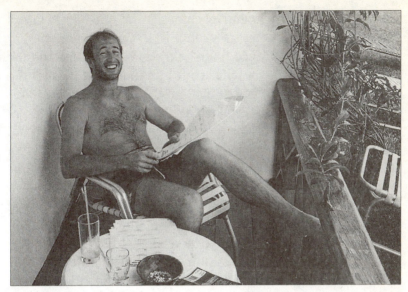

The things you do for your mates. It took me four days of trawling my photo albums to find a photo of Harry with a decent amount of hair.

if you do mate start investing in the two-litre bottles of sunscreen because you'll be needing every bit for that head of yours. Harry and I have been through heaps together over the years and he's one of my good cricketing buddies. **How could I ever forget his first series, when he was so nervous in a game against Australia at Eden Park that he was vomiting in the changing room and because of a migraine had to drop down the batting order?** I can still visualise Mark Plummer, our physio, draping cold towels over his forehead. Harry still gets strung up a little before he goes out to bat, and against Aussie at Cardiff he was bouncing off the walls and annoying the hell out of everyone. Harry also had a card school organised down the back of the bus, himself and Doully against the two youths, McMillan and Vettori. The youngsters are gamblers and there is always good wedge ($) up for grabs when they're around. Not that I'd trust them greatly either, and there were a number of accusations flying around the back of the bus on tour. Harry likes a punt and if there are any gaming machines at the hotel and Harry's missing, you'll know where to find him. Casinos are another retreat for H out of office hours, although he seemed to tuck this habit away once his wife arrived on tour. Like most of the guys, Harry is ultra-competitive, and it's on the golf course where many of his battles take place. He hits a big ball and I'm sure when he drives off the tee he has both feet off the ground. **Harry's always in demand with the media and when he's interviewed, the boys always count how many times H says the word 'obviously'. He hates it.**

It was a strange World Cup for Harry. He didn't get huge opportunities with the bat down at eight and only cranked out a couple of the not-outs that he's famous for. The bowling conditions also weren't tailor-made for H, with the May wickets in England suiting the quicks and the medium pacers, who hit the strings, rather than his rolling leg-spin deliveries. Accordingly, he was often left out of the attack by Flem until the 25-30 over stage, which meant he rarely bowled his sets of 10, and you could tell that frustrated Harry. But the conditions really dictated the bowling philosophy and Harry in effect shared the fifth bowler's quota with Nath.

Harry's a marvellous guy and as a team man he can't be bettered. The common phrase in the changing room is, 'Shut up Harry!' There's plenty of smiling when H is around.

Enjoys: Talking, golf, gambling, euchre, needing a haircut.

Geoff Allott

Well, what more can I say? Every tournament dream team I've seen named since the completion of the World Cup had GA cemented in at number 11 (sorry buddy, but I think they got the batting position correct). He was superb and continually got accolades from the media and the opposition, and that has to be a sign that you're doing things well. His comeback after serious injury and the resulting reconstruction of his bowling action is testimony to what the guy is all about. He deserved every success. And yet at the end of the tournament, and this sums up GA, he was disappointed. 'I let myself and the team down in the last match when they most needed me,' he said. GA, we wouldn't have got past the preliminary stages if it hadn't been for you.

I do have a bone to pick with him, though. On more than one occasion, he and Nashy met up to do their Body Control Pilates exercises without me. The deal at the start was the three of us together. **I guess they thought my 36-year-old abdominal muscles were in good enough nick. One of Karen's mates thinks GA looks like Richard Gere. Bloody hell, then I'm Tom Cruise.**

GA is a model team man, has fantastic talent, would spill his guts for the team, and has the desire to succeed. Give me 11 GAs and I'd have the World Cup at home with me now. Well done, mate.

Enjoys: Training, the physio table, chatting.

Daniel Vettori

Dan is 20 years old going on 30. This guy has the cricketing world at his fingertips. But please, Mr Fickle cricket media and public, remember that this front-line spinner is only 20. Dan was naturally gutted that he never got a chance in the World Cup, but never once did he drop his chin or his standards. As with all the 'dirties', he was great support throughout to the playing XI. If the tournament had been three months later, in drier conditions, then I'm positive Dan would have taken his spot and it could have been one of the batsmen, or myself, who made way. Dan and Macca are good mates, and can often be seen out drifting the streets or, more likely, heading to a local casino. **Recently Dan received official membership to the Christchurch Casino, which he had been kicked out of a number of times before he turned 20**.

Enjoys: The 'creased shirt' look, euchre, sleeping, batting.

Simon Doull

Another brilliant 'dirty' throughout this World Cup. I've been a dirty a few times myself, particularly when test match time rolls around, and it's the worst job in cricket. Our guys were really positive and kept supporting the whole way. **Doully would be seen most evenings with jeans and shirt on, heading out with mates that he was catching up with. He's certainly not one to bury himself away in his hotel room.** He's one of the world's great swing bowlers and I know he wants to take out his non-playing frustrations on the English test batsmen. Absolutely top-drawer in the allocating of the team match tickets.

Enjoys: Socialising, earrings, golf, goaties, euchre.

Carl Bulfin

The character of the team, as I'm sure you've worked out from the diary. At the last debrief Bully let us all know how disappointed he was not to make the test squad and vowed to go home, give it heaps, and prove a few people wrong. A great attitude. Not pleasant to face in the nets, particularly when he gets a bit fired up. Was hanging out for his girlfriend to arrive in England, then for a few days after was walking around like a peacock. Bully went for a half-hour run in Nottingham, took a wrong turning and promptly got lost. After questioning a local, he ended up doing a half-marathon to get back home. **Also not a great guy to room next to given his taste in music, which differs somewhat from my easy-listening and classical favourites.** Bully's work ethic on tour couldn't be faulted. If you poked your nose into the hotel gym, there he'd be, pumping some iron.

Enjoys: Heavy Metal, bowling fast, fitness training.

Matthew Hart

A good mate. Harty's really committed to making the team again and, like Bully, his work-ethic was spot-on. A top tourist who gets on with everyone, and when the time is right he makes a damned good 'going out' buddy. How could I forget the sound of Bully pinning him in the chest at the nets at The Oval? Ouch! Or the practice at Old Trafford when he tripped

MEET THE CAST

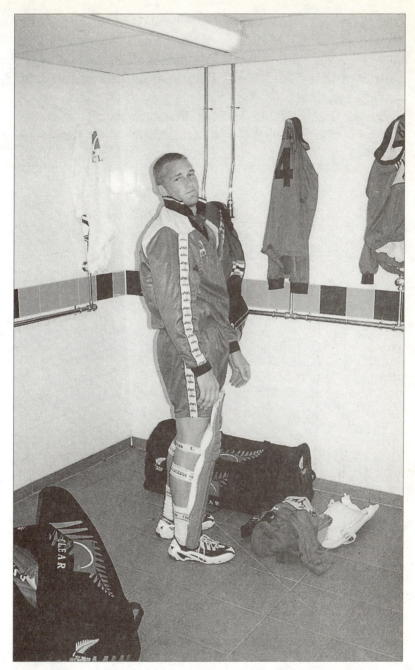

Bully with a 'smile'… you should see him when he's angry.

over the net, not once but twice, as he was delivering the ball? How could a man that unco-ordinated be a bowler? A great euchre player who showed commendable tolerance of his partner at times. And Harty, I enjoyed our pre-match euchre strategy meetings.

Enjoys: Receiving throw-downs (from me), socialising, euchre.

Anyone Can Dream

AFTER THE 1996 WORLD CUP, I had a testimonial season and as is traditional with that honour, I set about preparing a testimonial magazine. One of the features of that was writing a section on my team of the 1996 World Cup. Looking back at the team I chose, it is amazing how quickly the cricket world can turn around.

It was dominated by Sri Lankan players, understandable given their dominance of that event. But looking at doing the same job after this year's World Cup, there is not a Sri Lankan in sight. No Sanath Jayasuriya, no Aravinda de Silva and definitely no Arjuna Ranatunga, whom I chose as captain of that 1996 team. **The other interesting thing is that there are still no Englishmen in the team, and I guess that says something about their one-day play. At least this time I can squeeze in a New Zealander.**

There's no doubt that on their home pitches on the sub-continent, the Sri Lankans were a formidable foe. Their achievement in winning the World Cup in 1996 was outstanding, based as it was on some of the most fearsome batting imaginable. New Zealanders will recall how much we enjoyed the same approach four years earlier when Mark Greatbatch and Rod Latham gave us similar starts. It was really great for cricket here, and it was the same in Sri Lanka.

But this time around a whole tactical option was wiped out when the organisers decided to play with the Dukes make of ball.

GRAND LARSENY

Life at the top of the order became something of a luxury until the later weeks of the competition, when pitches firmed up.

The team I chose after 1996 was: Sanath Jayasuriya (Sri Lanka), Sachin Tendulkar (India), Mark Waugh (Australia), Aravinda de Silva (Sri Lanka), Brian Lara (West Indies), Arjuna Ranatunga (Sri Lanka, captain), Wasim Akram (Pakistan), Ian Healy (Australia), Shane Warne (Australia), Waqar Younis (Pakistan), Curtly Ambrose (West Indies).

The way Australia stormed home in England cannot help but make an impact in the selection. Mark Waugh and Adam Gilchrist struggled through the early stages, but when seven wins in seven games were needed by Australia, they started to rally to the cause, Waugh more than Gilchrist. I would have loved to put in the Zimbabwean Neil Johnson to open the innings. He was quite inspirational for the Zimbos and almost single-handedly saw them through to the Super Sixes with some great innings. **However, my selectorial head tells me that to balance the team Gilchrist needs to open the innings. His final assault on Pakistani speed man Shoaib Akhtar bears that out.** It also affects two other selections. Gilchrist's treatment of Shoaib helps his fast-bowling team-mate Glenn McGrath make the side at the Pakistani's expense and also means Moin Khan misses out as wicketkeeper with Gilchrist doing that job as well.

Sachin Tendulkar didn't dominate the Cup as many expected he would. It was fair enough for people to expect him to take charge. But the death of his father in the early stages, and the pressure on him as India looked to advance beyond the Super Six was unreal. However, there were still enough touches there for him to grace my team at No 3. He is definitely one player we enjoyed seeing the back of.

Choosing Rahul Dravid at No 4 will surprise no-one. For a player who was rubbished for not being a one-day batsman before he came to New Zealand at Christmas, he has certainly slammed his critics. A wonderful technician who can decimate the best attacks.

Jacques Kallis is going to be one of the world's great players,

ANYONE CAN DREAM

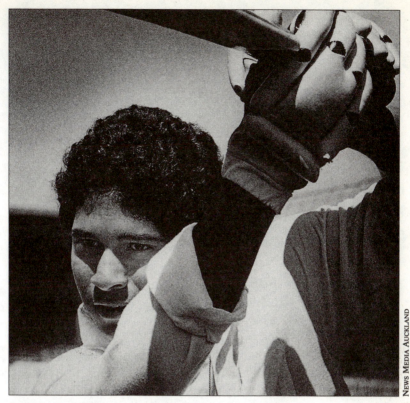

Sachin Tendulkar… graces my team at No 3.

if he isn't already. He is a dead cert for this team. Frontline batsman, opening bowler and athletic fieldsman. Kallis is a captain's dream, adding superb balance to the team. It was his first World Cup, but perhaps next time he might be part of a winning team. **The South Africans must wonder if they are ever going to win the World Cup.** They had that rain-affected semi-final at their first attempt in 1992, then they got upset by the West Indies in the quarter-finals in 1996, and now they stumbled in England. Being a Wellingtonian, I know how they must feel, on a much smaller scale of course!

Trying to stamp himself as a leader, a few months after succeeding one of the great all-time captains in Mark Taylor, Steve Waugh hasn't really put a foot wrong. But it was a close-

GRAND LARSENY

Steve Waugh... captains my World Cup team.

run thing. Australia came so close to tipping out of the competition early. I guess it is a sign of his leadership that Australia came through the way it did. And he played a huge role on his own by scoring that brilliant century in the Super Six game against South Africa, and then playing such a commanding role in the semi-final. **There were some who wondered about his one-day acumen - Martin Crowe for one - but Waugh has played too much one-day cricket not to have the ability to get himself out of most situations in the game. He'll do as captain for my World Cup team.**

Wasim Akram has been through the mill lately, more off the field than on, but despite all the turmoil around the Pakistanis, he moulded them into a highly-competitive unit who kept it all together until the very last moment. His bowling remains outstanding, he still wields a mean bat and is one player you can never relax against.

It is ironic that the man who stole the one-day series in New Zealand from us with that magnificent last ball six in Napier, Lance Klusener, should have been in the firing line with the scores tied at Edgbaston. But his batting throughout the series, backed with his style of bowling, makes him my first man selected. **He was clearly the player of the World Cup, and don't forget that great delivery that took his wicket for the first time in the World Cup!**

Shane Warne showed during the Cup what a magnificent bowler he is. Such was his impact on the game during the mid-90s, it would have been a great shame if his shoulder surgery had affected his ability to play again. If ever there was any doubt, it has been blown away now. He's back and he's doing the business. Not many spinners got a decent response from the Dukes ball in the World Cup, but I reckon Warne could turn a billiard ball on a billiard table.

Shoaib Akhtar had everyone watching the speed gun results whenever he bowled, and he was certainly too quick for some of our batsmen, but when it came to the absolute crunch, his inexperience was shown up by the Australians. He will be in many teams, but I have to go with Glenn McGrath, who is another big-hearted Aussie competitor. There's never any doubt where you stand with Glenn, just like Dennis Lillee and Merv Hughes. And just like them, he keeps on producing the great performances.

While the focus was on all the hot-shots in the lead-up to the Cup, our own Geoff Allott crept up and caught everyone by surprise. What a tournament he had. And what a hard worker who got the rewards for his efforts. His example is one that should inspire a whole new generation of players. His World Cup record of 20 wickets was thoroughly deserved. They can't criticise him either for the quality of the opposition. He did it day-in and day-out against some of the best in the world. In this selection, unfortunately, he remains in the dreaded No 11 spot.

So here's my 1999 World Cup team: Adam Gilchrist (Australia), Mark Waugh (Australia), Sachin Tendulkar (India), Rahul Dravid (India), Jacques Kallis (South Africa), Steve Waugh (Australia, captain), Wasim Akram (Pakistan), Lance Klusener (South Africa), Shane Warne (Australia), Geoff Allott (New Zealand), Glenn McGrath (Australia).

As I look back over a one-day career that has included three World Cups and the complete decade of the 1990s, I can't help but feel I have played through an outstanding era in the game. **There have been many champion players who have done battle with us Kiwis in New Zealand and overseas, and it has been a great privilege to pit our skills against them.** We have had our moments in New Zealand, and have shown we can be a very competitive side. And two semi-finals in three World Cups bears that out.

A team for the 1990s, considering players at the peak of their form, is a fascinating exercise. **My selection is:** Sanath Jayasuriya (Sri Lanka), Sachin Tendulkar (India), Mark Waugh (Australia), Martin Crowe (New Zealand), Brian Lara (West Indies), Steve Waugh (Australia), Wasim Akram (Pakistan), Lance Klusener (South Africa), Shane Warne (Australia), Waqar Younis (Pakistan), Curtly Ambrose (West Indies).

Martin's performance at the 1992 World Cup has to be one of the great efforts in our history. He was brilliant. His batting was so consistent and his captaincy almost unreal. Everything he did seemed to come off. It was just amazing to be part of it all, a very special part of New Zealand cricket history.

Sanath Jayasuriya revolutionised the first 15 overs of the game with his brilliant attacking play and while it didn't feature in 1999 in England, it is a tactic more likely than not to be employed in the future.

Waqar and Curtly are two fast bowling legends. Waqar for his brilliance with the speed he mustered and that damned reverse swing that makes life interesting down at the bottom of the batting order for blokes like me. Then there is Curtly, who had all that height advantage to play with. It was time to check the life insurance policies when they were in action.

True Colours

A CRICKET CAREER CAN take you to the Melbourne Cricket Ground, Lord's, Eden Gardens in India or Sharjah in the middle of the Arabian desert. But wherever you go, your travels always lead you home and, in cricket, home for me has always been Nairnville Park, Khandallah, Wellington. If there was ever a chance of becoming big-headed about some of the places I play the game, then returning to the grassroots is the perfect reminder of how fortunate I've been to experience the pleasures of international cricket.

Heaven help cricket if at the great grounds around the world you had to put up with the north-westerly wind regularly blowing the bails off, the ball thudding into batsmen's shins, and then next ball popping up into the chest region. That's not to forget the long-on fielder from the No 2 wicket fielding at short leg in the senior match on the No 1 wicket. **Also not to be overlooked is the corrugated iron-type outfield that makes the long barrier fielding technique a minimum requirement to avoid the embarrassment of the ball getting past you with a cruel bounce, even if the ball comes to you along the ground.**

It's all because like most other club cricket grounds in New Zealand, Nairnville Park, the home of Onslow Cricket Club, is a dual-purpose ground. It is used for both soccer and rugby in the winter and the way those sports churn up the ground in a wet winter makes club cricket in the summer especially interesting and challenging.

Wellington's cricket wickets have continually amazed me over the 20-odd years I've been involved in club cricket. Despite countless complaints to the ground authorities over the years from so many people involved in cricket, I cannot remember a club season where the wickets were ever any better than adequate. Getting more than a couple of hours' rolling on a pitch from a Wellington City Council groundsman is a luxury. **At Onslow we worked out once that by slipping the groundsman a dozen of beer on his back porch we could get an extra hour of rolling on the Friday before a match. We had the system perfected when the groundsman got sacked.** Apparently his neighbours weren't impressed with the marijuana he was cultivating in his back yard.

It did clarify a couple of things. We had been wondering why some or our clubmates seemed to prefer having a beer down at the groundsman's house than at the clubrooms. It also explained why there were a couple of weeks when the same guys managed to produce wickets that were 22 metres in length, instead of yards. That can make all the difference to some of the older bowlers in a side.

For all that, some of my most enjoyable, memorable and exciting cricket has been played around Wellington. While standards have ebbed and flowed over the years, there's no doubt that club cricket is played with a real competitive spirit. The merging of the Wellington and Hutt Valley senior competitions has added an extra edge. There has always been a big rivalry between the two associations. The 'Townies' or 'City Slickers', as we are called, have always battled to maintain superiority over the 'Boguns' from Struggletown. **The Hutt Valley players definitely aren't short of a word and in one of my few games for Onslow last season, a Hutt player asked me from second slip if I carried my Grecian 2000 in my toilet bag and if I parked my wheelchair in the changing room.**

But, if there's one game that ranks above all others, it is Onslow v Johnsonville, the local derby. During the 1980s and

'90s, it was a real grudge match played with spirit by some pretty competitive types. What made the game tougher for me was the treatment I got for crossing the tracks. I played all my junior cricket for the Village, as Johnsonville calls itself, and then went down to Onslow in my fourth-form year. It might have been more than 20 years ago, but the word loyalty is still thrown at me.

Talk about intense. In one game, Robbie Turner, a Village legend, was batting down at No 10 when he smashed the last ball of a one-dayer for six to win the match. He then ran a couple of laps in celebration. Robbie was never high on our Christmas card list, but he was a real competitor who was predictably unbearable upstairs over a beer later on.

In another game at Nairnville, the Village changing room was unfortunately locked and there wasn't a key in sight. While we all found it pretty amusing, the Village lads soon

The champion Onslow team of the late 1980s. From left: Andy Wilson, James O'Rourke, Dougal McLean, Andrew Cording, Mo Arthur, Gerald Jurie, Patrick O'Rourke, me, James Milne, Glenn Wilkinson, John Murtagh.

sorted it out – they just busted down the door and were soon out warming up with us. While I've relished every minute with Onslow, I've always followed the Johnsonville results with more than a passing interest and I admired their team of the 1980s. Hard-nosed guys like Stu Cater, Bruce Nelson, Nigel Blair, Alan Isaac (he of New Zealand Cricket fame), Don Newton, Derek Locke, Marc Warner and Ross Verry were the guts of their team. **They had a factor I love to see in any sports team – a real will to win. And they played it hard, very hard, and fair (most of the time).**

Some of the grounds in Wellington deserve mention.

Anderson Park: The home of Wellington Collegians. It is a beautiful ground set among the Botanical Gardens. There's no better spot in the middle of summer. If you fail early with the bat at least you can get in some quality sunbathing. The straight boundaries are incredibly short, probably about 40 metres, and a good top edge can fly into the rose bushes or over the fence, down the hill and into Bowen Street below, never to be seen again. Those short boundaries helped produce the first six of my senior career. I was 17 and in my first full season of senior club play was facing up to one Bruce Taylor, just coming to the end of his illustrious cricket career. He bounced me. I pulled out the hook shot (a rare sight that) but somehow hit the ball straight up in the air. **A strong southerly was blowing and the ball drifted down to fine leg, over the poorly-positioned fielder, and just cleared the short boundary. Tails just stood in mid-pitch scowling and shaking his head.**

Alex Moore Park and **Kilbirnie Park:** Two of the windiest grounds in the Capital and sometimes a nightmare for bowlers. Alex Moore is Johnsonville's home ground and because of its height up at the top of the Ngauranga Gorge, it can be a bit dicey when the low cloud cover rolls in. Kilbirnie is the home of Easts (the merged Kilbirnie and Midland-St Pat's clubs). At both grounds, the quick bowlers would be lining up to bowl downwind and any discussion on into-the-wind options generally ended up in my vicinity. Unfairly labelled, I reckon.

Certainly it was character building having to truck upwind for 20 overs a day. Mind you, the need for control has served me well during my international career.

But batsmen also have to be thinking about their options. One particularly windy day at Kilbirnie bore that out. Fred Beyeler, who played a few seasons for Wellington, was bowling with real pace downwind. The wicket was a bit dicey, and coupled with Fendooly's sometimes bent arm delivery [he was a champion javelin thrower at college], it definitely made me appreciate the wisdom of sticking around and facing the bowlers from the other end only. John Murtagh, a good mate, took most of Fendooly's deliveries that day, and ended with a number of bruises and welts all over his body. All in a good cause though, as I kept whacking the ball with the wind and managed a hundred in each innings. **To this day, Murts still thinks I didn't buy him enough beer that night.**

Kelburn Park: The home of the University Cricket Club is a picturesque ground next to Wellington's cable car with a great view over Wellington Harbour. One day at Kelburn, especially, sticks in my mind. I shared a 150-run partnership with Andy Wilson, one of the great Wellington club batsmen of all time. I scored 23. Andy that day played one of the best big-hitting innings I've seen in club cricket. He smashed his way to 160-odd and decimated the University attack. A couple of his sixes into the houses that overlook the ground were huge. There weren't too many singles run that day.

Onslow is typical of most clubs with its characters. Here are a few who have struck a special chord.

John Morrison and **Jeremy Coney:** Mystery Morrison was adamant that in club cricket his 'autumn leaves' style of bowling was the way to go. **He would attempt to lob the ball over the batsman on the full to land directly on top of the bails.** His success rate was minimal, but it was hilarious watching the batsmen attempt to improvise their shots to this delivery that would come down with ice on it. Things tend to be pretty basic with Mystery. He now does some rugby commentary work for a local TV company and in a recent Petone-Western Suburbs match it was obvious that he was struggling to pronounce the Samoan and Maori surnames. His comment at half-time was that he wished all the players were called Smith and Jones.

Listening to Mystery and Jerry holding court in the Onslow changing rooms will remain with me forever. Their cricketing tales were hilarious. This is why it is so important that our international players play club cricket when they can. As a 17-year-old, standing at third slip listening to two of my idols sharing stories was pretty special. For home games at Nairnville each member of the team would bring a plate of food and we'd share them around at the lunch break. Jerry's regular comment was, **'Damn, forgot to get anything.' He would then proceed to munch his way through most of my Mum's best bacon-and-egg pie. He's the best radio comments man by the length of the straight.**

Tim Vogel: Of Vogel House (Prime Minister's former residence in Lower Hutt) background. A good pedigree. Voges bowled left-arm medium (he said quick) and played a few games for Wellington. Always fronted for pre-season training with an incredible rub-on tan, then tried to convince the boys that he'd been wintering in Hawaii. Buys ostriches in his spare time.

James Milne: JD was proud to accept the honour of being one of the opposition's most hated senior cricketers. He had an ability to really get up an opponent's nose with his incessant talking and gamesmanship from behind the wickets. Developed the 'sneak-up-the-leg-side-and-stump-the-batsman-off-the-quick-bowler' delivery – not really in the spirit of the game, but that didn't concern him. A class keeper. If he'd lived anywhere other than Wellington (Erv McSweeney had a mortgage on the keeper's spot) he'd have played a lot of first-class cricket. **JD couldn't drink – one beer and he started talking Braille.** A lasting memory is a night at the club when he'd had more than one jug and was late heading home. His lady arrived and promptly dragged him out by the ear to the laughs of the guys.

Gerald Jurie: A top man is Gerry. He helped co-ordinate my testimonial season with Wellington a couple of years ago, giving so much of his time for nothing. A real competitor, and his Yugoslav blood certainly emerges in the heat of battle. A few years ago Gerry was in the middle of a slump; in fact, it was more of a horror trot. **He completed his fifth duck in a row one Saturday, stormed into the changing room, packed his gear, and promptly walked across Nairnville Park and home. Left us with 10 men.** This seventh retirement was a short one, ending the following Tuesday when he slunk back into practice. Has a fluctuating weight problem (like a lot of cricketers), not helped by his love of good food and terrible willpower. Great team and club man, his jug sculls down at Onslow are legendary.

Paddy and **Jimmy O'Rourke:** The brothers O'Rourke originated from Masterton which explains a lot of things. They brought some interesting habits with them over the hills. Paddy was a stalwart of the Wellington team for three seasons or so and carried our attack early in the '90s. Totally committed and aggressive. He would crawl over broken glass for the team. Had a huge temper, with four-letter word expletives often reverberating around Nairnville on Saturday afternoons. **In Jimmy's debut senior match, he was caught by a couple of team-mates relieving himself at mid-on between overs. His explanation? 'I couldn't wait until the lunch break.'** They were great team men who weren't scared of an ale or three.

Paul Christian: He's got no hammies, bad quads, concrete calves, a stiff groin, a broken back and stuffed shoulder. Fletch (Fletcher Christian, Mutiny on the Bounty, get it?) is a picture of athletic health. One thing drives Fletch, though. He won't retire until he's knocked off the record-holder for most senior wickets, yours truly. He sits in second place about 20 wickets behind me. Will be a great sight when we are both in our 50s, still pestering the captain for a bowl. A great off-spinner in his time, he played for Wellington B for a couple of season and would have challenged for the first-class team if Evan Gray hadn't been around the scene. Would be the most analytical cricketer I've met. He has a theory on everything, and enjoys sharing them over a pint and a roll-your-own fag.

Stu Bullen: Bomber has the worst throwing arm in the history of the game. I've seen my three-year-old daughter, Vanessa, throw her dolls further. Made gully his specialist fielding position so that he never had to throw more than 15 metres. Bomber has been a mate of mine since we played senior together as teenagers. A great one-day bowler, usually bowling his 10 overs of left-arm 'nude' spinners for about 20 runs. **He has always enjoyed a good cry, the best occasion being at his wedding, when he blubbed through the whole service with the best man (me) trying in vain to make a man of him.** Also coached the Johnsonville Central League soccer team to promotion a couple of years ago, and promptly cried at the after-match function.

John Murtagh: Inspirational captain who led from the front. Genuine all-rounder who once scored a hundred and took six wickets on the same day in club cricket. At one stage Murts would mountain bike everywhere, from one side of the city up to practice and then home afterwards. He captained the New Zealand under-19 team against the Aussies and I remember him arriving back at Onslow speaking with an Aussie twang. That soon got beaten out of him. And Murts, your analytical, rambling e-mails through the World Cup were top drawer.

Andy Wilson: A legend in Wellington club cricket. A great hard-hitting batsman and superb cover fieldsman (in his earlier days). Crap bowler, so crap that I actually had to drop a catch on purpose one day off his bowling – his success was really getting to me. With his glass of wine in one hand and cigar in the other, life wouldn't be the same without Drew strolling around the clubroom on a Saturday offering his opinions on the day's play. **Always manages to secure at least one of my annual two pairs of sponsored Adidas sunglasses for himself.**

That's the beauty about playing sport at the top level. Your club buddies will always let you know that you're just one of the boys. I've got good mates at Wellington and New Zealand level, but for sure the majority of my really enjoyable and memorable times have been with mighty Onslow.

Of Coaches And Captains

I'VE PLAYED UNDER A number of coaches and captains for New Zealand and it's fair to say that they have all had their own unique styles and idiosyncrasies. They had different strengths and weaknesses and I've enjoyed the company of them all. Wouldn't a world full of perfect people be boring? I'm in no doubt that mainly owing to the huge time commitments involved, coaching and captaining an international cricket team are two of the hardest, and often loneliest, jobs in sport.

As I'm sure all my team-mates would agree, I tend to get along with most people. I keep reasonably quiet within the team environment, don't rock the boat too much, and just attempt to get on and do my job as well as possible. Maybe at the odd time I'm a little too 'nice', not opinionated enough, and sit back a little too much. However, that's just me and my nature, and one of my big goals as a team member is to at all times respect everyone for who they are and what they can bring to the team. **As such, I feel that I've managed to maintain pretty sound relationships with all the coaches and captains I've played under.**

There is one thing I will take the liberty to mention here. Many players I've played with at New Zealand and provincial level have often used the coach and/or the captain as a crutch, someone they can easily blame for their own deficiencies. I'm a big believer in self-sufficiency. It's an absolute necessity if you want to be successful. You just won't survive in sport at these levels if you don't display this very important attribute, and it annoys the hell out of me when I see players pointing the finger at their coach or captain as an excuse for the way they are performing as an individual. **We have had some major dramas in New Zealand cricket in the time that I've been involved, and I feel they were often a result of people not having respect and tolerance for fellow humans,** and an inability or a reluctance to think for themselves and stand on their own two feet. It's been so heart-warming over these last three seasons to see such a dramatic improvement in these two areas, to a point where in this World Cup the feeling within our camp was the best that I've experienced. And it leaves me with a few warm fuzzies to think that when I leave the game shortly, we finally have our act together in this critical area. It doesn't guarantee success, but it's a pretty good start.

Here's a brief summary of the coaches and captains during my time with the New Zealand team:

Bob Cunis

My first coach back in 1989. Cunie was the ultimate salt-of-the-earth coach, a proud guy. I remember him in my first series extolling the virtues of 100 per cent guts and commitment, of crawling over broken glass for your country. He was a really effective seam bowler back in the 1960s and early '70s, and used to bowl a bit at practice off a couple of paces. **He couldn't run in any further because of a hip replacement he'd had. He still hit the seam and delighted in nicking out guys like Hogan or Jonesy.**

I played for a New Zealand XI against India at New Plymouth in 1990 (Tendulkar was there as a 16-year-old), and Cunie was the coach. He had been told to keep a close eye on the performances of Shane Thomson and Jonathan Millmow, who were competing for an opening bowling spot in the New Zealand team. Whenever they were bowling, he would be perched up behind the sightscreens at Pukekura Park watching closely; otherwise he could be found tucked away sleeping in the corner of the changing room. A fairly nocturnal coach, you could say.

Warren Lees
I first encountered Wal on the park as a 21-year-old playing for Wellington against Otago. Stephen Boock was bowling his left-armers, Bruce Blair and Stuart McCullum were fielding in close, right under my nose, and Wal was up close behind the sticks. To say I felt claustrophobic would be understating it. The talking was incessant, a lot of it quite humorous, and if the intention was to make me feel uncomfortable and intimidated, then it certainly worked. I was soon on my way, LBW to Boocky **('Don't play back, son. The arm ball will get you,' he used to say),** and Wal let me know that I was another young pretender who wouldn't bother them again.

That Otago team of the '80s was a really competitive unit. Wal controlled things from behind the stumps and it was

Me and Wally Lees, one of the great man managers.

obvious he had the total respect of his team-mates. That family type set-up was a major component of Wal's coaching style when he took over the reins of the New Zealand team. The 1992 World Cup team was a great example, and Wal and Hogan worked superbly together as coach and captain. They were innovative and proactive with their tactics, and Wal was always positive and continually cajoled and urged the guys forward. Someone like Murphy Su'a, who didn't play a game in the tournament, was always getting positive reinforcement from him. **Wal was certainly the best 'man-manager', if that's the right phrase, that I've encountered.**

I know the bomb episode in Sri Lanka really unsettled Wal. On one occasion when we were stuck in the hotel, unsure of the future of the tour, I was in Wal's room with a couple of the other players and Wal was quite cut up. He'd just rung home to find that his son had shut himself away in his bedroom cupboard, adamant that his dad was never returning home. No-one at all (or I should say, none of the players) blamed Wal for being one of the six who decided to head home, and to this day I'm sure that his decision was a huge factor in our losing a top coach soon after.

Geoff Howarth

Geoff has taken a lot of stick in the recent years about off-the-park issues, much of it now well-documented. What I do know is that Geoff had a strong philosophy on players being self-disciplined enough to know what was right and wrong for them in terms of their own game. **In other words, if a player wanted to have a few beers the night before the game to help him relax and unwind, and then turn in at say 11 o'clock, Geoff was comfortable with that.** I guess most of the players at times found that a little contradictory, particularly when Geoff turned up to the nets a bit surly and grumpy after a late night. Given the new systems and procedures now in place with the team, and the improvement in our consistency of performances, I'd have to say now that things were a little lax through this period.

My first tour with Geoff was in 1988 to Zimbabwe with the New Zealand Young Internationals. I can still remember Geoff's first chat to me, along the lines of, **'You won't find me loud or overbearing, and you might at times think that I'm not talking to you enough about your game. That's just the way I am. But if you've anything whatsoever you want to discuss with me just ask, my door is always open.'** He was true to his word and I remember a couple of long talks with him and Tony Blain about the philosophies and tactics of our great game. His cricket knowledge is huge. I really enjoyed that early tour with Geoff. It's strange sometimes how things pan out.

As an aside, that was the tour when at our first practice in Harare, Geoff asked Martin Pringle (from Auckland, no relation to Chris), to bowl seamers in one of the nets. Pring had become a bit of a mate through cricket, and had previously shared with me that he was really surprised to have been picked for the tour. His surprise was perhaps justified by Geoff's request, for he discovered that he'd been picked for the tour as an all-rounder, though he was actually a top-order batsman for Auckland and bowled only very occasionally. Who said the selectors always get it right? Still, it was good for me. I got plenty of bowling on that tour.

John Reid

Reido took over the coaching reins in a caretaker capacity during the turbulent 1995 Centenary Season. It was an unenviable job but one that Reido attacked in his normal fashion. **He started by instilling some of the systems and disciplines that had been so badly missing previously.** He outlined his expectations which were definitely in line with the way he played his cricket, with commitment, loyalty, and plenty of hard work. With his playing background, Reido was also invaluable in terms of his technical knowledge and what was required at the top level. I know many of the batsmen enjoyed their work with Reido, and I for one would have been most comfortable if he had taken a longer term in charge.

Glenn Turner

I was really looking forward to my first meeting with Glenn Turner, the coach. It was held at the Wellington Cricket Association offices, and I had over an hour with him. Before this meeting I'd never had the opportunity to talk with Turns at length, and was excited to find out where his philosophies lay. He came prepared. Out of his briefcase he pulled a wad of paper, which was a detailed statistical breakdown of my career. Being armed with averages, RPOs, and strike-rates was just a start. He also had wagon-wheels pulled together and we talked through things such as in what areas of the ground batsmen were taking runs off me, the percentage of boundaries versus ones and twos, and my results when bowling to left and right-handed batsmen. He also didn't neglect the longer version of the game, which was music to my ears. It was the first time any coach had made an initial analysis of my game in this fashion.

The big thing that Turns stressed to me was the requirement for self-sufficiency from his players, and for them to have the ability to think for themselves. That became one of his trademarks. I enjoyed Turns as a coach, which is certainly different to how some players would describe their relationships with him. I guess if I was to sum up myself, it's that I've been pretty much self-contained over the years and haven't needed a hell of a lot of external advice. When I needed thoughts or guidance, I'd just go and ask the pertinent person. And I haven't needed much reinforcement, cajoling, or massaging from captains or coaches. That's probably why I had no problems with Turns. Against the West Indies in Guyana in '96, I bowled a really good spell in a low-scoring match that we won by four runs. It was a superb victory. Turns was sitting quietly in the corner of the changing room at the end. I caught his eye, and he nodded and winked. That was all. That was Turns. He wasn't big on praise. That was a fact, and some players hated that. To be fair, Turns was quite ruthless at times. Craig Spearman scored his debut test century at Eden Park in '96, and, after having the Zim bowlers at his mercy, got out for 112. The boys were rapt

Is that a letter from Chris Doig, Glenn? Lee Germon and Turns, India 1995.

for him, congratulating him back in the hutch. When Turns entered, he patted Spears on the shoulder and simply said, 'Well, you blew a double hundred there, eh?' Ouch! He wasn't flexible in this area and that can't be good. If a guy needs to have a little extra positive reinforcement, or to have his ego massaged a bit to get the best out of him, so what? And why not? No two players are exactly the same and we all have different ways of operating.

Turns was adamant that the first 15 overs in one-dayers were the key. Early wickets when bowling and a hefty strike rate when batting. His attitude was that he'd rather be bowled out for 260 with five overs left as opposed to being conservative and ending with say 230. He was willing to lose up to four wickets in the first 15 as he felt that we had a long batting order, which had the ability to recover from bad starts. That was true, and in the West Indies in the two one-dayers we played at Trinidad, I batted at 11 and every guy had scored a first-class hundred. He never wanted us to die wondering. He did take it to extremes, though. The sixth and final ODI in Bombay in '97 was a good case. We lost early wickets on a wicket that was going sideways, and never recovered. I went in when we were 97-7 with about 25 overs still to be bowled. His advice to me was, 'Get yourself in and then play your shots. There's no point only getting 170 because that won't win the game.' I saw what he was saying, but didn't agree. Back in Guyana we had defended 158, and my feeling is that you should always attempt to use up the 50 overs, and to scramble through to whatever is possible. Not Turns, though.

Inside that tough and astute cricket mind is also a real humanitarian. I could never forget a great gesture he made in Delhi. He has a strong Indian background through his wife, Sukhi. During his many visits to Delhi he got to know an Indian family well, a mother and her children who took up residence in some local public toilets next to the Taj Hotel, where the team stayed. He took it upon himself to help relocate the family to better surroundings in Delhi. He paid for the new accommodation himself, and physically helped the family relocate. A couple of the boys assisted Turns, and I'll never forget the look on their faces. Fantastic.

Steve Rixon
My first one-on-one meeting with Stumper went along the following lines. 'Mate, I've got huge respect for what you've achieved in New Zealand cricket, but I have to tell you, I don't see you having any role whatsoever in test cricket while I'm the coach, as my philosophy lies with using attacking bowlers. But as long as my butt points down, you're fit and in form, then you'll be in my one-day team every time.' **I certainly knew where I stood with Stumper from day one. While I didn't agree with his test philosophy, I admired the up-front and honest manner of the new coach.** And during his reign, that's what we've got from Stumper – frankness and honesty. He calls a spade a spade and there's one thing I can swear to: while he's Australian, he's had a Kiwi heart for the last three years.

OF COACHES AND CAPTAINS

Stumper (right) with BA and Flem.

Stumper has bought a new dimension to fielding in New Zealand with his variety of intensive fielding drills. As a result of the huge emphasis he places on fielding, the consistency of our fielding has never been better. Right from the start he said that fielding would be the difference in many of our games, and he was proved correct. One good thing from a player's perspective is that he has become less intense at practice the day before match day, and at warm-ups pre-match. I remember one particular warm-up at the MCG before a Carlton and United match. It was 38 degrees and after fielding drills that seemed to go forever, I was absolutely shagged. And I still had a 50-over one-day international in front of me!

Stumper never misses a ball bowled in any match. He sets himself up, usually in the corner of the viewing area, pen and paper in hand, and is right at home if the sun is out. One thing's for sure: the boys know the times to avoid sitting by the coach.

New Zealand has fashioned a good record under Stumper, and that's testimony to a greater degree of toughness he has engendered in the players and, most importantly, a greater self-belief within the individuals. The Australian influence has to an extent rubbed off on the boys, and that may be Stumper's legacy to New Zealand cricket.

Jeff Crowe
Chopper was skipper in my first series, but I honestly can't remember my own play let alone what the leader was like. **I was so nervous, and was concerned only about the degree of sledging I was receiving from the Aussies. I copped an earful from Healy, Waugh and Co as normally happens to the new boys.** My only real recollections of Chopper were as a batsman, elegant and stylish. A great hundred for Auckland against Wellington at the Basin when I chased leather all day springs to mind.

John Wright
My main memory of Wrig is of him sitting in the corner of the old changing rooms at Eden Park, having scored 60-odd against Australia, wearing only long white Y-fronts and dragging on a smoke. Wrig the captain seemed quite laid-back, but I'm sure that was a facade. Inside I'm sure he was stewing, which was always the impression I got about his batting. He was never happy with his bats, and was forever picking up new ones, looking for that ideal piece of willow. **I remember one period when I must have tossed Wrig 10,000 throwdowns as he searched for that ideal straight drive.** A quite brilliant team man. His team-talks were inspiring and always laced with a patriotic theme.

There were two guys who really helped me feel comfortable when I first made the team – Wrig and Martin Snedden. Both appeared to go out of their way to make me feel at home, but now I know that attitude was just inherent in their nature. It was as natural to them as it is unnatural to others. They certainly made me feel welcome. Wrig was my roomy in Melbourne during a World Series match and I found out that he hated noise. He had us moved from the fourth floor to the 21st, to avoid the traffic noise from the street below. Here I was rooming with one of my idols, and I could hardly dare to breathe in the bed next to him.

Martin Crowe

The greatest batsman I've ever had the privilege to play with. It was a real honour to play alongside Hogan for both Wellington and New Zealand. He was sheer class and so far ahead of any of our other batsmen it wasn't funny. Hogan was brilliant tactically when he held the reins. It was almost as if he was playing human chess. **He knew the game inside out and the basics were easy to him. It was when he played his gut-felt hunches that he proved quite inspirational.** The '92 World Cup was a classic example... spinner opening the bowling, the first 15 overs of aggressive batting, short rotations of the bowlers, hunches with field placements, and his inspirational lead-from-the-front batting. That six-week campaign was the highlight of my career. In retrospect, of my three World Cups, this was the one we could have, and should have, won. Seven wins on the trot in the lead-up, and then THAT semi-final against the Pakistanis at Eden Park. That damned hamstring tear of Hogan's will go with us all to our graves!

Ken Rutherford

I'll tell you one guy I would have loved in our top order at this World Cup – my old mate Kenneth Rutherford. His involvement with New Zealand cricket was definitely cut short and his best international years were still in front of him when he was cast into the wilderness. It annoys me that South African cricket is reaping the benefits of his experience. He has scored over 13,000 first-class runs now, has 27 hundreds, averages 40, and last season for Gauteng he scored 886 first-class runs at 59.06. Damned good stats those. It's such a shame that so much baggage surrounds Ruds after his unsavoury departure from New Zealand cricket.

Rudder is a mega-talented batsman. His gutsy street-fighting style is what makes him so valuable, and I remember some sensational innings when he tore the Wellington attack apart. We shared many good times together and he was a great guy socially. Glenn Turner called him a Public Bar cricketer at one point (there

GRAND LARSENY

Ken Rutherford... what a boon he would have been at the '99 World Cup.

seemed to be no love lost between those two), and certainly sitting in a bar with a pint of Speights in one hand, a racebook in the other, and watching *Trackside* was his idea of heaven.

His Batman impersonation one night on tour in Zimbabwe will remain with me forever. We were at a poolside barbecue, plenty of invited guests were milling around, and Rudder found himself a New Zealand flag. **Well, off came his clothes, the flag was wrapped around him, and he charged around the party introducing himself to all the locals as 'Bat-Rudder'!**

I really enjoyed his captaincy. He was astute and played his hunches really well and his good tactical nous nearly brought us a famous test victory at Lord's in 1994. Only bad light stopped our charge for victory. He was a players' skipper. The formal meetings were fine, but his best calls were often 'meeting this evening, 7pm in the bar for an hour'.

Lee Germon
I've read and listened to a lot a crap about Germ's captaincy

OF COACHES AND CAPTAINS

over the last couple of years. Some people have suggested that he was Glenn Turner's puppet. If you got to know Germ well enough, you'd soon learn that he was no-one's puppet. His tactical appreciation of the game was right up there with Hogan's, and he was a very strong individual. I listened in a number of times as Germ and Turns bounced ideas off each other, and there was no doubt in my mind that Germ was his own man, and that the coach and captain had a really good working relationship.

Germ didn't suffer fools lightly, and with a few personal agendas floating around during his time in charge, it made for a few stand-offs that didn't help anyone. **The hardest task Germ had was gaining the respect of a number of the players when he was given the skipper's job with basically no international experience behind him.** That didn't sit well with some of the players, and that particular knife was pointed at him for the duration of his reign – no matter what was happening on the park. Some of the guys continued to say that Germ was too much in management's camp, but, to be fair, it must have been bloody hard on him when he knew he had no chance whatsoever of gaining the respect of some of the players. When he walked away from the New Zealand game, I was left with a feeling that once again cricket had lost a valuable experienced player far too early.

Germ's team meetings were always well-structured. He was articulate, he analysed the opposition well, and the guys' roles were always well spelt out. **He was also willing to lead from the front, throwing himself up the order a number of times in an effort to create a strike rate in the first 15 overs of the one-day games.** And who could forget the partnership that he and Harry shared in the '96 World Cup quarter-final against Australia in Madras, which enabled us to get through to 286-9 after being 40-3? It was brilliant stuff.

Stephen Fleming
Flem's captaincy is going from strength to strength and both as a player and as a captain he should be the lynchpin around

which our team is built in future years. I remember Stumper saying to me during Flem's first series as captain something along these lines, 'One of my big goals as coach is to assist Flem's development to a point that when I leave as coach he is totally self-sufficient'. He then said to me with a smile during this World Cup, 'That time has arrived'.

My big hope, along with every cricket supporter I'd guess, is that we see Flem continue to develop into the world-class top-order batsman that we know he can be, and that the captaincy doesn't inhibit that progress at all. He is a batsman right out of the top drawer and we all have our fingers crossed that the captaincy complements his class batting.

Moving On Out

DURING MY TESTIMONIAL SEASON with Wellington in 1997, the song *Moving On Up* by M People became my song. It was the song I walked out to when batting, and was the song we selected to be the background music to my testimonial video. I guess now if there was a *Moving On Out*, that would be pertinent. **The 1999-2000 season will be my last season of cricket at all levels. It's time to move on out, and start a new chapter in life.** It's been a great time, and writing this book has brought so many memories flooding back. Right now, I've still got the desire to be on the park and competing at all levels, to make personal contributions and to win games. And I'll approach this season as I've approached every other one, with total commitment. I will finish off my career playing for whomever I am selected for. And then, come April 2000, it'll be time to move on.

I certainly have some unfinished business with Wellington. I dread to think how many finals we've reached in the '90s without going the whole way. And then there is the new stadium. A fantastic new facility in the best city in New Zealand. I played my last international on the Basin Reserve last summer. Being part of the first cricket team to play in the new stadium would also be something quite special to me.

The other thing that dawned on me as I wrote this small closing was that it will also be my last season for Onslow. Twenty-two years of club cricket. Last season we got relegated to the second division, and no disrespect intended, but won't it bring a smile to the face if my last outing in competitive cricket is for the mighty Onslow against say Upper Hutt at Maidstone Park No 2.

In closing off the book, there was one offering to the treasure chest during the World Cup that I thought was just great. It was The Kiwi Badge and it was donated by the one and only DJ Graham, who when placing it in the chest made a quite inspiring speech. It was summarised by Bert in the following manner, and I know everyone who reads this will identify with it in some way:

The Kiwi Badge

This became the symbol of our New Zealand Expeditionary Force (NZEF) in the second World War. It gained special significance in the North African campaign where Rommel's German army was halted at El Alamein – a fortress on a hill in North Africa. It was there that a heavily outnumbered and outgunned contingent of NZ, Australian, and English forces took the fortress after a bitter and intense battle. It was this battle that turned the African campaign and resulted in Rommel's retreat.

The badge represents:
- fortitude and strength against great odds
- total resilience and confidence in those around you
- pride in your nation and the determination to defend those at home
- belief in your values
- the relish of personal and collective challenges.

Stats

ONE-DAY INTERNATIONALS

Season	v	M	I	NO	HS	Runs	Ave	100	50	ct	Overs	Mdns	Runs	Wkts	Ave	Best	RPO
1989/90	TRI	5	3	0	1	2	0.66	-	-	1	43.1	2	169	2	84.50	1-14	3.91
1990/91	WS	2	1	0	6	6	6.00	-	-	-	18	3	68	0	-	-	3.77
1990/91	SL	3	-	-	-	-	-	-	-	1	30	4	98	4	24.50	2-25	3.26
1990/91	E	3	2	2	10*	11	-	-	-	-	29	1	110	1	110.00	1-35	3.79
1991/92	E	3	1	1	3*	3	-	-	-	-	25	6	94	3	31.33	2-24	3.76
1991/92	WC	9	2	1	37	45	45.00	-	-	5	76	7	262	9	29.11	3-16	3.44
1992/93	Z	2	-	-	-	-	-	-	-	-	16	0	78	0	-	-	4.87
1992/93	P	3	1	0	11	11	11.00	-	-	-	29	4	65	3	21.66	2-15	2.24
1992/93	A	5	5	3	33*	94	47.00	-	-	-	49	6	163	4	40.75	3-17	3.32
1993/94	WS	7	7	4	29*	83	27.66	-	-	-	64	6	250	2	125.00	2-12	3.91
1993/94	P	5	4	1	9*	21	7.00	-	-	-	45	3	129	8	16.12	4-24	2.86
1993/94	I	4	2	0	5	7	3.50	-	-	1	30	2	134	3	44.66	1-33	4.46
1993/94	AAC	3	3	3	18*	41	-	-	-	-	29	1	147	1	147.00	1-34	5.06
1994	E	1	1	0	13	13	13.00	-	-	-	10	1	43	0	-	-	4.30
1994/95	WI	3	2	0	15	27	13.50	-	-	-	27	5	104	2	52.00	1-35	3.85
1994/95	NZC	4	3	1	3	5	2.50	-	-	1	32	2	128	4	32.00	3-39	4.00
1994/95	SL	3	1	1	2*	2	-	-	-	1	26	1	107	2	53.50	2-20	4.11
1995/96	I	5	3	1	20	31	15.50	-	-	1	46.5	4	190	4	47.50	2-40	4.08
1995/96	P	4	4	2	23	42	21.00	-	-	-	39	0	157	5	31.40	2-42	4.02
1995/96	Z	2	-	-	-	-	-	-	-	1	18	5	56	4	14.00	3-42	3.11
1995/96	WC	2	1	0	1	1	1.00	-	-	1	18	2	74	3	24.66	2-33	4.11
1995/96	WI	5	2	0	9	10	5.00	-	-	-	46.4	10	146	9	16.22	3-26	3.12
1996/97	SIC	1	1	0	0	0	0.00	-	-	-	9	1	22	1	22.00	1-22	2.44
1996/97	E	5	4	1	19	33	11.00	-	-	1	41.3	0	155	7	22.14	3-20	3.73
1996/97	SL	2	2	0	26	39	19.50	-	-	1	12	5	32	1	32.00	1-23	2.66
1996/97	IC	3	3	1	12	14	7.00	-	-	-	27.3	3	115	6	19.16	3-43	4.18
1997/98	Z	3	1	0	16	16	16.00	-	-	2	27	0	116	4	29.00	2-42	4.29
1997/98	CUS	4	2	1	0*	0	0.00	-	-	1	27.4	1	110	5	22.00	3-56	3.97
1998/99	I	5	2	1	12	14	14.00	-	-	3	43	1	203	6	33.83	2-34	4.72
1998/99	SA	7	4	1	17*	27	9.00	-	-	1	51	2	212	4	53.00	2-39	4.16
1999	WC	8	3	2	14	30	30.00	-	-	1	76	3	263	6	43.83	3-19	3.46
TOTAL		121	70	27	37	629	14.62	-	-	23	1061.2	91	4000	113	35.39	4-24	3.76

Key to tournaments: WC – World Cup, **WS** – World Series, **AAC** – Austral-Asia Cup, **SC** – Sharjah Cup, **SIC** – Singer Cup, **NZC** – New Zealand Centenary, **IC** – Independence Cup, **CUS** – Carlton & United Series, **TRI** – Triangular Tournament.

1999 WORLD CUP
Top Ten Economical Bowlers (min 25 overs)

		Overs	Mdns	Runs	Wkts	Ave	Best	RPO
C.A. Walsh	(WI)	47	8	108	11	9.81	4-25	2.30
C.E.L. Ambrose	(WI)	40	6	94	7	13.42	3-31	2.35
R.D. King	(WI)	31.3	4	95	8	11.87	3-30	3.01
S.M. Pollock	(SA)	84	11	283	9	31.44	5-36	3.37
G.R. Larsen	(NZ)	76	3	263	6	43.83	3-19	3.46
Monjurul Islam	(B)	27	4	94	3	31.33	2-33	3.48
P.V. Simmons	(WI)	39	5	136	5	27.20	2-33	3.49
A.D. Mullally	(E)	50	6	176	10	17.60	4-37	3.52
S. Elworthy	(SA)	72	9	262	10	26.20	2-20	3.64
Muralidaran	(SL)	43	3	158	6	26.33	3-25	3.67

SHELL CUP

Season	M	I	NO	HS	Runs	Ave	100	50	ct	Overs	Mdns	Runs	Wkts	Ave	5W	Best	RPO
1984/85	4	4	1	26	45	15.00	-	-	1	39	2	135	6	22.50	-	2-23	3.46
1985/86	4	2	1	3*	3	3.00	-	-	1	26	2	73	2	36.50	-	2-22	2.80
1987/88	5	5	0	66	107	21.40	-	1	3	43	3	124	6	20.66	-	3-28	2.88
1988/89	5	4	1	26	43	14.33	-	-	2	25.2	1	102	3	34.00	-	2-50	4.02
1989/90	6	5	1	45	90	22.50	-	-	2	54	8	162	5	32.40	-	2-16	3.00
1990/91	7	6	2	26	108	27.00	-	-	4	62.4	7	173	11	15.72	-	4-27	2.76
1991/92	6	6	3	29*	54	18.00	-	-	-	49	4	139	1	139.00	-	1-20	2.83
1992/93	6	6	1	39	100	20.00	-	-	2	54	14	126	4	31.50	-	2-6	2.33
1993/94	4	3	1	11	24	12.00	-	-	-	29	4	104	2	52.00	-	1-15	3.58
1994/95	13	8	0	33	97	12.12	-	-	4	124.3	18	361	10	36.10	-	3-10	2.89
1995/96	9	9	3	44	144	24.00	-	-	8	87.3	11	312	10	31.20	1	5-30	3.57
1996/97	11	9	2	38*	103	14.71	-	-	3	101.4	20	298	21	14.19	-	3-21	2.93
1998/99	7	6	2	40	135	33.75	-	-	4	70	9	225	13	17.30	-	4-28	3.21
TOTAL	87	73	18	66	1053	19.14	-	1	34	765.4	103	2334	94	24.82	-	5-30	3.05

TEST MATCHES

Season	v	M	I	NO	HS	Runs	Ave	100	50	ct	Overs	Mdns	Runs	Wkts	Ave	5W	10W	Best
1994	E	1	2	0	8	10	5.00	-	-	2	44.4	11	116	2	58.00	-	-	2-116
1994/95	SA	1	2	1	26*	27	27.00	-	-	-	42.3	13	88	5	17.60	-	-	3-57
1994/95	SL	2	3	1	21*	37	18.50	-	-	3	94.4	35	173	7	24.71	-	-	3-73
1995/96	P	1	2	1	13	18	18.00	-	-	-	44	12	102	4	25.52	-	-	2-43
1995/96	Z	1	1	0	0	0	0.00	-	-	-	26	11	38	1	38.00	-	-	1-30
1995/96	WI	2	3	1	17*	35	17.50	-	-	-	76	27	172	5	34.40	-	-	3-76
TOTAL		8	13	4	26*	127	14.11	-	-	5	327.5	109	689	24	28.70	-	-	3-57